RICHARD NORTON-TAYLOR

Educated at King's School, Canterbury, Oxford University and
the College of Europe, Bruges, Richard Norton-Taylor wrote
for the *Washington Post*, *Newsweek*, *Financial Times* and
Economist before joining the *Guardian* in 1975. Since then, he
has investigated official secrecy, behind-the-scenes decision-
making in Whitehall and the activities of the security and
intelligence services. He has regularly contributed to radio
and television.

Prior to editing the *Nuremberg War Crimes Trial* for presen-
tation at the Tricycle Theatre, London, Richard Norton-Taylor
(together with John McGrath) wrote *Half the Picture*, an adap-
tation of the Scott 'Arms to Iraq' Inquiry, which was presented
at the Tricycle Theatre, Houses of Parliament and on BBC-2.
Richard received a 1994 Freedom of Information Campaign
Award for *Half the Picture*, which also won a 1994 Time Out
Drama Award.

His books include: *Whose Land is it Anyway: an Investigation
into Land Ownership*; *The Ponting Affair*; *Blacklist: the
Inside Story of Political Vetting* (with Mark Hollingsworth);
*In Defence of the Realm? The Case for Accountable Security
and Intelligence Services*; *A Conflict of Loyalties: GCHQ,
1984-1991* (with Hugh Lanning), *Truth is a Difficult Concept:
Inside the Scott Inquiry*, and *Knee Deep in Dishonour* (with
Mark Lloyd and Stephen Cook).

He won the 1986 Freedom of Information Campaign Award
and is a member of the Civil Liberties Trust and the London
Action Trust.

NUREMBERG

THE WAR CRIMES TRIAL

transcript edited by
RICHARD NORTON-TAYLOR

*with additional documentary material
compiled by*
Nicolas Kent and Richard Norton-Taylor

NICK HERN BOOKS
London

A Nick Hern Book

Nuremberg – The War Crimes Trial first published in Great Britain
in 1997 as a paperback original by Nick Hern Books,
14 Larden Road, London W3 7ST

Typeset by Country Setting, Woodchurch, Kent TN26 3TB
Printed by Athenaeum Press Ltd, Gateshead, Tyne and Wear

A CIP catalogue for this book is available from the British Library

ISBN 1 85459 332 3

And while the West laid itself open to the charge of appease-ment – as it has done since, in response to atrocities elsewhere, most recently in the former Yugoslavia – the Soviet Union was also culpable. It had attacked Poland, Finland and the Baltic States at the beginning of the War. It took Moscow fifty years to admit responsibility for the massacre – for at Nuremberg it blamed the Nazis – of nearly 15,000 Polish officers, including those killed in the Katyn Forest in Byelorussia. And there were Stalin's gulags . . .

Nuremberg prosecutors laid themselves open to the charge that they were indulging in victors' justice. The Allies were vulnerable to the 'dirty hands' defence – that they were conveniently ignoring their own actions. Lord Shawcross confesses in his recent memoirs *Life Sentence* (Constable) to be worried by the 'historical view that by their own conduct of the war, the Allies had lost the moral authority to conduct the trial. I have always felt it was difficult to defend our saturation bombing of Dresden and Hamburg at a time when Germany was already collapsing. I have felt a similar difficulty about the atom bombing of Hiroshima and Nagasaki – especially if, as is now believed by some, this horrific demonstration was intended not so much to bring an early end to the war with Japan as to warn the Soviet Union of the power available to the West.'

The very title of the Tribunal – of German Major War Criminals – gave away its limitations. The world had to wait, notably for the Eichmann trial, for a fuller, more complete picture. It showed, as Destexhe puts it, 'how the overall plan to exterminate the Jews was part of a huge bureaucratic process, a mosaic of minuscule fragments, each one individually very ordinary and commonplace . . . Only a tiny percentage of those who participated in the genocide actually shot a Jew or turned on the gas. It was the bureaucrats who helped to destroy the Jewish people, often whilst remaining at their desks. Gassing rather than shooting was an ingenious system which avoided any one person being directly responsible for an actual killing'. Of the tens of thousands estimated by Lord Shawcross as having committed crimes which, he says, 'cried out for punishment', a few hundred were sentenced to death by the four victorious powers.

Contents

Introduction
The Legacy of Nuremberg vii
The Nuremberg War Crimes Trial, 1946 x
The Defendants xii
Convictions and Sentences xiv

Cast List xvi

Nuremberg: The War Crimes Trial 1

Sir Hartley Shawcross: After Nuremberg . . . 57
Justice Richard Goldstone: Address 59

Appendix
Notes on the Defendants 65
Notes on the Evidence 69

INTRODUCTION

The Legacy of Nuremberg

The core crimes were genocide and crimes against
Rudolf Hoess, first commandant of Auschwitz – wh
as a witness for Kaltenbrunner whose counsel hope
client's role would look relatively mild in comparis
apparent insouciance described in detail the search
more efficient measures of gassing its inmates. (Ho
hanged in April 1947 in the grounds of Auschwitz.
after his capture in 1946 that he believed three milli
had died in the camp. Though he later lowered his e
1.13 million, US prosecutors at Nuremberg used the
three to four million.)

But the transcripts of the trial show how relatively l
was devoted to these atrocities which raised uncom
questions. As Alain Destexhe says in his book, *Rwa
Genocide in the Twentieth Century* (Pluto Press): 'L
Second World War, at no time did the Allies modify
military objectives in order to save Jews, even after
when there was no longer any possible doubt as to v
happening. Half a million Jews were murdered in A
between March and November 1944, when the last
took place, yet the railway lines leading to the death
were never targeted.'

The Nuremberg Trial became bogged down in lengt
arguments about Counts One and Two whose proble
compounded by Jackson's ineffective cross-examina
in particular of Goering, who showed himself to be a
confident defendant. Counts One and Two caused di
for the Allies. As E.L. Woodward, historical adviser
Foreign Office, told Whitehall: 'Up to September 1s
His Majesty's Government was prepared to condone
Germany had done to secure her position in Europe.'

INTRODUCTION

The Legacy of Nuremberg

The core crimes were genocide and crimes against humanity. Rudolf Hoess, first commandant of Auschwitz – who appeared as a witness for Kaltenbrunner whose counsel hoped his client's role would look relatively mild in comparison – with apparent insouciance described in detail the search for ever more efficient measures of gassing its inmates. (Hoess was hanged in April 1947 in the grounds of Auschwitz. He said after his capture in 1946 that he believed three million people had died in the camp. Though he later lowered his estimate to 1.13 million, US prosecutors at Nuremberg used the figure of three to four million.)

But the transcripts of the trial show how relatively little time was devoted to these atrocities which raised uncomfortable questions. As Alain Destexhe says in his book, *Rwanda and Genocide in the Twentieth Century* (Pluto Press): 'During the Second World War, at no time did the Allies modify their military objectives in order to save Jews, even after 1944 when there was no longer any possible doubt as to what was happening. Half a million Jews were murdered in Auschwitz between March and November 1944, when the last gassings took place, yet the railway lines leading to the death camps were never targeted.'

The Nuremberg Trial became bogged down in lengthy arguments about Counts One and Two whose problems were compounded by Jackson's ineffective cross-examinations, in particular of Goering, who showed himself to be a clever and confident defendant. Counts One and Two caused difficulties for the Allies. As E.L. Woodward, historical adviser to the Foreign Office, told Whitehall: 'Up to September 1st, 1939, His Majesty's Government was prepared to condone everything Germany had done to secure her position in Europe.'

And while the West laid itself open to the charge of appease-
ment – as it has done since, in response to atrocities elsewhere,
most recently in the former Yugoslavia – the Soviet Union was
also culpable. It had attacked Poland, Finland and the Baltic
States at the beginning of the War. It took Moscow fifty years
to admit responsibility for the massacre – for at Nuremberg it
blamed the Nazis – of nearly 15,000 Polish officers, including
those killed in the Katyn Forest in Byelorussia. And there were
Stalin's gulags . . .

Nuremberg prosecutors laid themselves open to the charge
that they were indulging in victors' justice. The Allies were
vulnerable to the 'dirty hands' defence – that they were
conveniently ignoring their own actions. Lord Shawcross
confesses in his recent memoirs *Life Sentence* (Constable) to
be worried by the 'historical view that by their own conduct of
the war, the Allies had lost the moral authority to conduct the
trial. I have always felt it was difficult to defend our saturation
bombing of Dresden and Hamburg at a time when Germany
was already collapsing. I have felt a similar difficulty about the
atom bombing of Hiroshima and Nagasaki – especially if, as is
now believed by some, this horrific demonstration was intended
not so much to bring an early end to the war with Japan as to
warn the Soviet Union of the power available to the West.'

The very title of the Tribunal – of German Major War
Criminals – gave away its limitations. The world had to wait,
notably for the Eichmann trial, for a fuller, more complete
picture. It showed, as Destexhe puts it, 'how the overall plan to
exterminate the Jews was part of a huge bureaucratic process,
a mosaic of minuscule fragments, each one individually very
ordinary and commonplace . . . Only a tiny percentage of those
who participated in the genocide actually shot a Jew or turned
on the gas. It was the bureaucrats who helped to destroy the
Jewish people, often whilst remaining at their desks. Gassing
rather than shooting was an ingenious system which avoided
any one person being directly responsible for an actual killing'.
Of the tens of thousands estimated by Lord Shawcross as
having committed crimes which, he says, 'cried out for
punishment', a few hundred were sentenced to death by the
four victorious powers.

Contents

Introduction
   The Legacy of Nuremberg   vii
   The Nuremberg War Crimes Trial, 1946   x
   The Defendants   xii
   Convictions and Sentences   xiv

Cast List   xvi

Nuremberg: The War Crimes Trial   1

Sir Hartley Shawcross: After Nuremberg . . .   57
Justice Richard Goldstone: Address   59

Appendix
   Notes on the Defendants   65
   Notes on the Evidence   69

The Defendants

Karl Doenitz
Commander of the German Navy, appointed Chancellor in
May 1945 after Hitler's death

Hans Frank
Governor-General of Poland

Wilhelm Frick
Reich Minister of the Interior and Protector of Bohemia and
Moravia

Hans Fritzsche
A Reich Ministry of Propaganda official

Walther Funk
President of the Reichsbank

Hermann Goering
Hitler's successor-designate in September 1939, Chairman of
the Reich Council for National Defence and Commander of the
Luftwaffe

Rudolf Hess
Hitler's former deputy who flew to Britain in 1941 with a peace
offer, apparently on his own accord

Alfred Jodl
Chief of the Wehrmacht Operations Staff

Ernst Kaltenbrunner
Chief of the Reich Security Department

Wilhelm Keitel
Chief of Staff of the Wehrmacht

Constantin von Neurath
Former Protector of Bohemia and Moravia and Minister
without Portfolio

Count Three charged the defendants with committing war crimes between September 1939 and 8 May 1945, including the murder and ill-treatment of civilian populations of occupied territories, murder and ill-treatment of prisoners of war, killing of hostages, plunder of public and private property, exacting collective penalties, wanton destruction not justified by military necessity, conscription of civil labour and 'Germanisation' of occupied territories.

Count Four charged the defendants with the commission of crimes against humanity in Austria, Czechoslovakia and in Germany itself prior to May 1945 and in all countries occupied by German armed forces after 1 September 1939. The crimes cited included murder, extermination, enslavement, deportation and persecution of political, racial and religious groups.

The prosecuting countries divided up the counts between them: the US was given responsibility for Count One – the conspiracy charge; Britain for Count Two; and the French and Russians dealt with the Third and Fourth Counts in, respectively, Western and Eastern Europe.

All the defendants, who could choose their own counsel, pleaded not guilty. A not guilty plea was entered for Martin Bormann in his absence. Robert Ley, Director of the Labour Front, hanged himself in his cell shortly before the trial started. Ernst Kaltenbrunner, Chief of the Reich Security Department, who was in hospital at the start of the trial after a stroke, later made a personal plea of not guilty. Gustav Krupp, the industrialist, was too ill to face trial. Hitler – the Führer, Himmler – Head of the SS, and Goebbels – Head of the Reich Ministry of Propaganda, had all committed suicide before the trial. The proceedings were simultaneously translated into four languages – English, Russian, French and German. The official transcript runs to about six million words. The prosecution called 33 witnesses, the defendants called 61. Over 50 million pages of documents were produced at the trial.

The Nuremberg War Crimes Trial, 1946

The Nuremberg Trial of German Major War Criminals opened amid great fanfare and rhetoric on 20 November 1945. More than ten months later, on 1 October 1946, of the twenty-two defendants, twelve were sentenced to death by hanging – Martin Bormann in absentia – three were sentenced to life imprisonment, four were sentenced to prison terms ranging from ten to twenty years, and three were acquitted. Goering committed suicide by swallowing a cyanide capsule shortly before he was due to be hanged.

There were four judges with one alternate from each of the victorious powers, with Britain's Lord Justice Lawrence serving as President: the Russian member of the Tribunal, General Nikitchenko, gave a dissenting opinion against the acquittal of three of the defendants, the refusal to sentence Rudolf Hess (not to be confused with Hoess) to death, and against the majority decision to acquit the Reich Cabinet and the General Staff and High Command of the German armed forces of being criminal organisations.

The Tribunal was established by Britain, the US, France and the Soviet Union (with the support of Governments-in-exile whose countries were occupied by Germany) under a Charter indicting both individuals and organisations, not only for war crimes and crimes against humanity, but also for crimes against peace and for conspiring in a common plan.

Count One charged the defendants, over a ten-year period up to May 1945, with participating in a common plan or conspiracy to commit crimes against peace, war crimes and crimes against humanity as defined in the Charter.

Count Two charged them over the same period with crimes against peace – participating in the planning, preparation, initiating, and waging wars of aggression.

In Britain, The War Crimes Act of 1991 is an admission of Whitehall's failure or reluctance to vet those implicated from coming to Britain. Anthony Glees, historian and adviser to the inquiry that led to the Act, estimates that there are about 100 'serious suspects' still alive in Britain.

Shawcross confidently predicted at Nuremberg that the Tribunal would 'provide a contemporary touchstone and an authoritative and impartial record to which future historians may turn for truth, and future politicians for warning'. Fifty years later, these words have a hollow ring in the light of war crimes perpetuated by the Nuremberg victors – the bombing of Cambodia during the Vietnam War, for example, or the treatment of Algerians fighting for independence. (The US writer Noam Chomsky, has said: 'If the Nuremberg laws were applied, then every postwar American President would have been hanged.')

Yet even those who accept that the Nuremberg Trial was flawed insist that nevertheless it remains deeply significant. 'For the first time,' says David Cesarani, Professor of Modern Jewish Studies at Manchester University, 'individuals were put on trial for sending their people to war and ordering them to commit atrocities . . . it was no longer enough to say: "We were just obeying orders." '

Now, for the first time since Nuremberg, the UN has set up war crimes tribunals – for the former Yugoslavia and Rwanda. Richard Goldstone, the South African judge and first chief prosecutor at both of the tribunals, has described them as 'a major step ushering in a new era in the history of international law and especially international humanitarian law.' Like Shawcross, he is pressing for a permanent international war crimes tribunal.

Richard Norton-Taylor

Franz von Papen
Former Chancellor of Germany

Erich Raeder
Former Commander-in-Chief of the German Navy

Joachim von Ribbentrop
Foreign Minister

Alfred Rosenberg
Minister for the Occupied Eastern Territories and the Nazi
Party's official 'philosopher' – his book *The Myth of the
Twentieth Century* was a best-seller – and the propagator of
crude anti-Semitism

Fritz Sauckel
Plenipotentiary for Labour Mobilisation

Hjalmar Schacht
Former Minister of Economics and President of the Reichsbank

Baldur von Schirach
Reich Youth Leader

Arthur Seyss-Inquart
Reich Commissioner in the Netherlands

Albert Speer
Minister of Armaments and War Production

Julius Streicher
Former Gauleiter of Franconia and founding editor of *Der
Stürmer*, a rabidly anti-Semitic newspaper

Martin Bormann
Head of the Nazi Party Chancellery – tried in absentia

Convictions and Sentences

All the defendants pleaded not guilty

Defendant	Count One	Count Two
Martin Bormann	not guilty	not charged
Karl Doenitz	not guilty	guilty
Hans Frank	not guilty	not charged
Wilhelm Frick	not guilty	guilty
Hans Fritzsche	not guilty	not charged
Walther Funk	not guilty	guilty
Hermann Goering	guilty	guilty
Rudolf Hess	guilty	guilty
Alfred Jodl	guilty	guilty
Ernst Kaltenbrunner	not guilty	not charged
Wilhelm Keitel	guilty	guilty
Erich Raeder	guilty	guilty
Joachim von Ribbentrop	guilty	guilty
Alfred Rosenberg	guilty	guilty
Fritz Sauckel	not guilty	not guilty
Hjalmar Schacht	not guilty	not guilty
Arthur Seyss-Inquart	not guilty	guilty
Albert Speer	not guilty	not guilty
Julius Streicher	not guilty	not charged
Constantin von Neurath	guilty	guilty
Franz von Papen	not guilty	not guilty
Baldur von Schirach	not guilty	not charged

Count Three	Count Four	Sentence
guilty	guilty	death
guilty	not charged	ten years
guilty	guilty	death
guilty	guilty	death
not guilty	not guilty	acquitted
guilty	guilty	life imprisonment
guilty	guilty	death
not guilty	not guilty	life imprisonment
guilty	guilty	death
guilty	guilty	death
guilty	guilty	death
guilty	not charged	life imprisonment
guilty	guilty	death
guilty	guilty	death
guilty	guilty	death
not charged	not charged	acquitted
guilty	guilty	death
guilty	guilty	twenty years
not charged	guilty	death
guilty	guilty	fifteen years
not charged	not charged	acquitted
not charged	guilty	twenty years

Nuremberg was first presented on stage together with *Ex-Yu* by Goran Stefanovski, *Haiti* by Keith Reddin and *Reel Rwanda* by Femi Osofisan, at the Tricycle Theatre, London, in May-June 1996, with the following cast:

Mr Justice Robert H. Jackson
Chief Prosecutor for the US   Colin Bruce

Sir Hartley Shawcross, *H.M. Attorney General,*
Chief Prosecutor for the UK   Richard Heffer

General R.A Rudenko
Chief Prosecutor for the USSR   Mark Powley

Lord Justice Lawrence
President of the Tribunal   David Webb

Reichsmarschall Hermann Goering
Commander of the Luftwaffe
and Hitler's designated successor   Michael Cochrane

Dr Stahmer, *Counsel for Goering*   Hugh Simon

Sir David Maxwell-Fyfe
Deputy Chief Prosecutor for the UK   Mark Penfold

Field-Marshal Wilhelm Keitel
Chief of the Staff of the Wehrmacht   William Hoyland

Dr Otto Nelte, *Counsel for Keitel*   Raad Rawi

Rudolf Hoess, *Commandant of Auschwitz*   Thomas Wheatley

Dr Kurt Kauffmann
Counsel for Kaltenbrunner   James Woolley

Alfred Rosenberg
Reich Minister for Eastern Occupied Territories   Jeremy Clyde

Dr Thoma, *Counsel for Rosenberg*   Mark Penfold

Mr Thomas Dodd, *US Assistant Prosecutor*   Raad Rawi

Albert Speer
Minister of Armaments and War Production   Michael Culver

Dr Hans Flaeschner, *Counsel for Speer*   Hugh Simon

Director Nicolas Kent

Set Designer Saul Radomsky

Costume Designer Jacqueline Abrahams

Lighting Designer Simon Opie

The production was revived with the same cast in September-October 1996, together with *Srebrenica* edited by Nicolas Kent, which was an account of the Rule 61 hearings against Dr Karadzic and General Mladic at the International War Crimes Tribunal in The Hague.

In the Tricycle production, the words used by Francis Biddle were spoken by the President of the Tribunal.

Nuremberg was commissioned from an idea by Nicolas Kent for the Tricycle Theatre in 1995.

NUREMBERG

The court pioneered the use of a simultaneous translation system. A red light on the prosecutors' and witnesses' boxes stopped proceedings and a yellow light signalled the speaker to slow down.

MR JUSTICE ROBERT H. JACKSON (*Chief Prosecutor for the United States of America*). The privilege of opening the first trial in history for crimes against the peace of the world imposes a grave responsibility. The wrongs which we seek to condemn and punish have been so calculated, so malignant, and so devastating, that civilisation cannot tolerate their being ignored, because it cannot survive their being repeated.

That four great nations, flushed with victory and stung with injury, stay the hands of vengeance and voluntarily submit their captive enemies to the judgement of the law, is one of the most significant tributes that Power ever has paid to Reason.

We must never forget that the record on which we judge these defendants today is the record on which history will judge us tomorrow. To pass these defendants a poisoned chalice is to put it to our lips as well.

We would also make clear that we have no purpose to incriminate the whole German people. We know that the Nazi Party was not put in power by a majority of the German vote.

These defendants were men of a station and rank which does not soil its own hands with blood. They were men who knew how to use lesser folk as tools.

The most savage and numerous crimes committed by the Nazis were those against the Jews.

Of the nine million, six hundred thousand Jews who lived in Nazi-dominated Europe, 60 percent are authoritatively estimated to have perished. History does not record a crime ever perpetrated against so many victims nor one ever carried out with such calculated cruelty.

'Undesirables' were exterminated by injection of drugs into the bloodstream, by asphyxiation in gas chambers. They were shot with poison bullets, to study the effects.

I am one who received, during this war, most atrocity tales with suspicion and scepticism. But the proof here will be so overwhelming that I venture to predict that not one word I have spoken will be denied. These defendants will only deny personal responsibility or knowledge.

The Third Count of the Indictment is based on the definition of War Crimes contained in the Charter. It will appear, for example, that the defendant Keitel was informed by official legal advisers that the orders to brand Russian prisoners of war, to shackle British prisoners of war, and to execute Commando prisoners were clear violations of International Law. Nevertheless, these orders were put into effect.

The Fourth Count of the Indictment is based on Crimes against Humanity. Chief among these are mass killings of countless human beings in cold blood. Does it take these men by surprise that murder is treated as a crime?

The First and Second Counts of the Indictment add to these crimes the crime of plotting and waging wars of aggression. The idea that a State, any more than a corporation, commits crimes, is a fiction. Crimes always are committed only by persons.

The Charter recognises that one who has committed criminal acts may not take refuge in superior orders nor in the doctrine that his crimes were acts of State.

PRESIDENT. I will now call upon the Chief Prosecutor for the United Kingdom of Great Britain and Northern Ireland.

HM ATTORNEY-GENERAL, SIR HARTLEY SHAWCROSS (*chief prosecutor for the United Kingdom of Great Britain and Northern Ireland*). By agreement between the Chief Prosecutors, it is my task – on behalf of the British Government, and of the other States associated in this prosecution to present the case on Count Two of the Indictment and to show how these defendants, in conspiracy with each other and with persons not now before this Tribunal, planned and waged a war of aggression in breach of the Treaty obligations by which, under International Law, Germany, as other States, had sought to make such wars impossible.

Under the General Treaty for the Renunciation of War of 27th August, 1928, practically the whole civilised world abolished war as a legally permissible means of enforcing the law or changing it. The right of war was no longer of the essence of sovereignty.

Let us see how these defendants, Ministers and High Officers of the Nazi Government, individually and collectively, comported themselves in these matters.

On 1st September, 1939, in the early hours of the morning, under manufactured and, in any event, inadequate pretexts, the armed forces of the German Reich invaded Poland along the whole length of her frontiers and thus launched the war which was to bring down so many of the pillars of our civilisation.

As early as August 1938, steps were being made to utilise the Low Countries as defence bases for decisive action in the West in the event of France and England opposing Germany in the aggressive plan on foot against Czechoslovakia.

On the 10th May, 1940, at about 0500 hours in the morning, the German invasion of Belgium, Holland and Luxemburg began. The only fault of these unhappy countries was that they stood in the path of the German invader in his designs against England and France. But that was enough.

On the 6th of April, 1941, German forces invaded Greece and Yugoslavia.

On the 22nd of June, 1941, the German armed forces invaded Russia, without warning, without declaration of war. The Nazi armies were flung against the power with which Hitler had so recently sworn friendship, and Germany embarked upon that last act of aggression in Europe which, after long and bitter fighting, was eventually to result in Germany's own collapse.

It is indeed true, as Great Britain fully accepts, that immediately a State accepts international obligations it limits its sovereignty. In that way, and that way alone, lies the future peace of the world.

The government of a totalitarian country may be carried on without representatives of the people, but it cannot be carried on without any assistance at all. It is no use having a leader unless there are also people willing and ready to serve their personal greed and ambition by helping and following him.

It is no excuse for the common thief to say, 'I stole because I was told to steal', for the murderer to plead, 'I killed because I was asked to kill'. And these men are in no different position. Political loyalty, military obedience, are excellent things, but they neither require nor do they justify the commission of patently wicked acts. There comes a point where a man must refuse to answer to his leader if he is also to answer to his conscience. Even the common soldier, serving in the ranks of his army, is not called upon to obey illegal orders.

If these crimes were in one sense the crimes of Nazi Germany, they also are guilty as the individuals who aided, abetted, counselled, procured and made possible the commission of what was done.

GENERAL R.A.RUDENKO (*Chief Prosecutor for the Union of Soviet Socialist Republics*). Having prepared and carried out the perfidious assault against the freedom-loving nations, fascist Germany turned the war into a system of militarised banditry.

The murder of war prisoners, extermination of civilian populations, plunder of occupied territories and other war crimes were committed as part of a totalitarian lightning war programme – 'Blitzkreig' – projected by the fascists. In particular, the terrorism practised by the fascists on the temporarily-occupied Soviet territories reached fabulous proportions and was carried out with fiendish cruelty.

'We must', said Hitler, 'pursue a policy of systematic depopulation. If you ask me what I mean by the term "depopulation", I would tell you that I understand it to be the complete removal of whole racial groups. And that is what I am going to do; such, roughly, is my purpose.'

The names have already been mentioned here of the concentration camps, with their gas chambers. The Germans also carried out mass shootings of Soviet citizens. The mass murders, this arbitrary regime of terror, was fully approved by the defendant Rosenberg in a speech in November 1942:

'If we are to subjugate all these peoples (ie peoples inhabiting the territory of the USSR) then arbitrary rule and tyranny will be an extremely suitable form of Government.'

In April, 1942, a top secret circular, 'Programme of the General-Plenipotentiary for the Employment of Labour' was sent. It noted that 'it is extremely necessary fully to utilise the human reserves available in occupied Soviet territories'. 400,000 to 500,000 'selected, healthy and strong girls' were ordered to be brought to Germany from the eastern Territories 'in order that the burden on the overworked German peasant woman should be noticeably lightened'.

The German fascist invaders completely or partially destroyed or burnt 1,170 cities and more than 70,000 villages and hamlets; they burnt or destroyed over 6 million buildings and rendered some 25 million persons homeless.

Himmler mentioned that it was necessary to cut down the number of Slavs by 30 million.

Now, when as a result of the heroic struggle of the Red Army and of the Allied Forces, Hitlerite Germany is broken and overwhelmed, we have no right to forget the victims who have suffered.

May justice be done !

THE PRESIDENT. Will you give your name please?

GOERING (*Commander in Chief of the Air Force and successor-designate to Hitler*). Hermann Goering.

THE PRESIDENT. Will you repeat this oath after me: I swear by God the Almighty and Omniscient that I will speak the pure truth and will withhold and add nothing.

The witness repeated the oath.

THE PRESIDENT. You may sit down if you wish. Dr Stahmer do you wish to examine the defendant?

DR STAHMER. When were you born and where?

GOERING. I was born on 12th January, 1893, in Rosenheim, Bavaria.

STAHMER. Give the Tribunal a short account of your life up to the outbreak of the First World War, but briefly, please.

GOERING. Normal education, first tutored at home; then cadet corps, then an active officer. A few points which are significant with relation to my later development: the position of my father as first Governor of South-West Africa, his connections at that time, especially with two British statesmen, Cecil Rhodes and the elder Chamberlain . . .

STAHMER. Tell the Tribunal when and under what circumstances you came to know Hitler?

GOERING. After the collapse in the First World War, I settled down in the neighbourhood of Munich . . . I found out I could hear Hitler speak, as he held a meeting every Monday evening. Finally, I saw a man here who had a clear and definite aim.

He gave me for the first time a very wonderful and profound explanation of the concept of National Socialism; the uniting of the concept of Nationalism on the one hand and Socialism on the other, which could prove itself the absolute bearer of Socialism as well as Nationalism, the Nationalism, if I may say so, of the bourgeois world and the Socialism of the Marxist world.

In the middle of 1932, after numerous elections had taken place, we became the strongest Party, and I was elected President of the Reichstag, and thereby took over a definite political task.

Then in January, 1933, there were further elections. One must not forget that at this moment Germany had arrived at the lowest point of her downward development, 8 million unemployed; all programmes had failed; no more confidence in the Parties; a very strong rise on the part of the revolutionary Leftist side; and political insecurity.

In the end, we were the strongest Party with 232 seats.

At 11 o'clock in the morning of the 22nd January 1933, the Cabinet was formed and Hitler appointed Reich Chancellor.

STAHMER. What measures were taken to strengthen Hitler's power?

GOERING. The Führer told me that the simplest thing to do would be to take as example the United States of America, where the Head of State is at the same time the Head of the Government. That he thereby automatically became also the Commander-in-Chief of the German Armed Forces followed as a matter of course, according to the Constitution.

STAHMER. Did you create the Gestapo, and the concentration camps?

GOERING. For the consolidation of power, the first prerequisite was to create along new lines that instrument which at all times and in all nations is always the inner political instrument of power, namely the police. There was no Reich police. In order to make clear from the outset that the task of of this police was to make the State secure, I called it the Secret State Police.

STAHMER. The concentration camps?

GOERING. When the need for creating order, first of all, and removing the most dangerous element of disorder directed against us now became evident, I reached the decision to have the Communist functionaries and leaders arrested all at once.

STAHMER. The Party Programme included two points dealing with the question of the Jews. What was your basic attitude towards this question?

GOERING. The Nuremberg Laws were intended to bring about a clear separation of races and, in particular, to do away with the concept of a person of mixed blood in the future . . .

STAHMER. You said you had been considered the Führer's successor. Were you in this capacity included in all political problems by Hitler?

GOERING. Of course, he informed me of all important political and military problems.

PRESIDENT. Do the Chief Prosecutors wish to cross-examine?

MR JUSTICE JACKSON. You are perhaps aware that you are the only living man who can expound to us the true purposes of the Nazi Party and the inner workings of its leadership?

GOERING. I am perfectly aware of that.

JACKSON. You, from the very beginning, together with those who were associated with you, intended to overthrow, and later did overthrow, the Weimar Republic?

GOERING. That was, as far as I am concerned, my firm intention.

JACKSON. And, upon coming to power, you immediately abolished parliamentary government in Germany?

GOERING. We found it to be no longer necessary. Also I should like to emphasise the fact that we were, moreover, the strongest parliamentary party and had the majority. But you are correct when you say parliamentary procedure was done away with because the various parties were disbanded and forbidden.

The people were merely to acknowledge the authority of the Führer or, let us say, to declare themselves in agreement with the Führer. Thus, not the individual persons were to be selected according to the will of the people, but solely the leadership itself.

JACKSON. After you came to power, you regarded it necessary, in order to maintain power, to suppress all opposition parties?

GOERING. We found it necessary not to permit any more opposition, yes.

JACKSON. And you also held it necessary that you should suppress all individual opposition lest it should develop into a Party of Opposition?

GOERING. In so far as opposition seriously hampered our work of building up, this opposition of individual persons was, of course, not tolerated.

JACKSON. Now, in order to make sure that you suppressed the parties, and individuals also, you found it necessary to have a secret political police to detect opposition?

GOERING. I have already stated that I considered that necessary, similar to the former political police, but on a firmer basis and larger scale.

JACKSON. And upon coming to power you also considered it immediately necessary to establish concentration camps to take care of your incorrigible opponents?

GOERING. The reason for the concentration camps was not because it could be said, 'Here are a number of people who are opposed to us and they must be taken into protective custody'. Rather they were set up as an emergency measure against the functionaries of the Communist Party who were attacking us in their thousands and who, since they were taken into protective custody, were not put in prison.

JACKSON. But you are explaining, as the high authority of this system, to men who do not understand it very well; and I want to know what was necessary to run the kind of system that you set up in Germany. The concentration camp was one of the things you found immediately necessary upon coming into power, was it not? And you set them up as a matter of necessity, as you saw it?

GOERING. That was faultily translated – it went too fast. But I believe I understood the sense of your remarks. You asked me if I considered it necessary to establish concentration camps immediately in order to eliminate opposition. Is that correct?

JACKSON. Your answer is, 'Yes', I take it?

GOERING. Yes.

JACKSON. Protective custody meant that you were taking people into custody who had not committed any crime but who, you thought, might possibly commit a crime?

GOERING. Yes. People were arrested and taken into protective custody who had not yet committed any crime, but who could be expected to do so if they remained free, just as similar protective measures are being taken in Germany today on a tremendous scale.

JACKSON. Now, it is also a necessity, in the kind of State that you had, that you have some kind of organisation to carry propaganda down to the people and to get their reaction and inform the leadership of it, is it not?

GOERING. The last part of that question has not been intelligibly translated.

JACKSON. Well, you had to have organisations to carry out orders and to carry your propaganda in that kind of State, did you not?

GOERING. Of course we carried on propaganda, and for this we had a propaganda organisation.

JACKSON. And you carried that on through the Leadership Corps of the Nazi Party, did you not?

GOERING. The Leadership Corps was there, of course, partly to spread our ideas among the people. Secondly, its purpose was to lead and organise the people.

JACKSON. When was it State necessity to kill somebody, you had to have somebody to do it, did you not?

GOERING. Yes, just as in other States; whether it is called Secret Service or something else, I do not know.

JACKSON. And the SS, organisations of that kind, were the organisations that carried out the orders and dealt with people on a physical level, were they not?

GOERING. The SS never received an order to kill anybody, not in my time. Anyhow I had no influence on it . . . I know that orders were given for executions, and these were carried out by the police, that is by a State organ.

JACKSON. What police?

GOERING. As far as I can recall, through the Gestapo. At any rate, that was the organisation that received the order. You see, it was a fight against enemies of the State.

JACKSON. The SS carried out all the functions of the camps, did they not?

GOERING. If a SS unit was guarding a camp and an SS leader happened to be the camp commander, then this unit carried out all the functions.

JACKSON. As to organisation, everybody knew what the Gestapo was, did they not?

GOERING. Yes, everyone knew what the Gestapo was.

JACKSON. And what its programme was, in general, not in detail?

GOERING. I explained that programme clearly. At the very beginning, I described that publicly, and I also spoke publicly of the tasks of the Gestapo, and I even wrote about it for foreign countries.

JACKSON. And there was nothing secret about the establishment of a Gestapo as a political police, about the fact that people were taken into protective custody, about the fact that there were concentration camps? Nothing secret about those things, was there?

GOERING. There was at first nothing secret about it at all.

JACKSON. As a matter of fact, part of the effectiveness of a secret police and part of the effectiveness of concentration camp penalties is that the people do know that there are such agencies, is it not?

GOERING. It is true that everyone knows that if he acts against the State he will end up in a concentration camp, or will be accused of high treason before a court, according to the degree of his crime. But the original reason for creating the concentration camps was to keep there those people whom we rightfully considered enemies of the State.

JACKSON. Now, is that type of government – the government which we have just been describing – the only type of government which you think is necessary to govern Germany?

GOERING. I should not like to say that the basic characteristic of this government and its most essential feature was the immediate setting up of the Gestapo and the concentration camps in order to take care of our opponents. Over and above that we had set down as our government programme a great many, much more important, things and those other things were not the basic principles of our government.

JACKSON. But all those things were necessary things, as I understood you, for purposes of protection?

GOERING. Yes, these things were necessary because of the opponents that existed.

JACKSON. And I assume that that is the only kind of government that you think can function in Germany under present conditions?

GOERING. Under the conditions existing at that time, it was, in my opinion, the only possible form, and it also demonstrated that Germany could be raised in a short time from the depths of misery, poverty and unemployment to relative prosperity.

JACKSON. Now, all this authority of the State was concentrated? Perhaps I am taking up another subject . . .

You have related to us the manner in which you and others co-operated in concentrating all authority in the German State in the hands of the Führer; is that right?

GOERING. I was speaking about myself and to what extent I had a part in it.

JACKSON. Is there any defendant in the box you know of, who did not co-operate toward that end so far as was possible?

GOERING. That none of the defendants here opposed or obstructed the Führer in the beginning is clear.

JACKSON. By January 1945 . . . there was no way to prevent the war going on as long as Hitler was the head of the German Government, was there?

GOERING. As long as Hitler was the Führer of the German people, he alone decided whether the war was to go on. As long as my enemy threatens me and demands absolutely unconditional surrender, and held out those terrible conditions which had been intimated, I would have continued fighting whatever the circumstances.

SIR DAVID MAXWELL FYFE (*deputy chief prosecutor for the UK*). Will you look at the document, Document D-728, Exhibit GB 282. Witness, I want you to deal with the sentence in paragraph 6, 'the administration, enlargement, installations and deterrent tasks in the concentration camps must be destroyed at all costs. Also the extermination of some families etc. These files must under no circumstances fall into the hands of the enemy, since they are, after all, secret orders by the Führer'.

Now this paragraph is certainly directed to all administrative levels down to the county leaders of the Nazi Party, and it assumes they knew all about the running of concentration camps. Are you telling the tribunal that you, who up to 1943 were the second man in the Reich, knew nothing about concentration camps?

GOERING. First of all, I want to say that I do not accept this document and that its whole wording is unknown to me and that this paragraph seems unusual to me. I did not know anything about what took place and the methods used in the concentration camps until later, when I was no longer in charge.

FYFE. Let me remind you of the evidence that has been given before this Court, that as far as Auschwitz alone is concerned, 4 million people were exterminated. Do you remember that? Are you telling this tribunal that a Minister with your power in the Reich could remain ignorant that that was going on?

GOERING. These things were kept secret from me. I might add that, in my opinion, not even the Führer knew the extent of what was going on.

FYFE. But, witness, had you not access to the foreign Press, the Press Department in your Ministry, to foreign broadcasts? You see, there is evidence that altogether, when you take the Jews and other people, something like 10 million people have been done to death in cold blood, apart from those killed in battle. Something like 10 million people. Do you say that you never saw or heard from the foreign Press, in broadcasts, that this was going on?

GOERING. First of all, the figure 10 million is not established in any way. Secondly throughout the war I did not read the foreign Press because I considered it nothing but propaganda. Thirdly, though I had the right to listen to foreign broadcasts, I never did so, simply because I did not want to listen to propaganda. Neither did I listen to home propaganda.

FYFE. The Führer, at any rate, must have had full knowledge of what was happening with regard to concentration camps, the treatment of the Jews, and the treatment of the workers, must he not?

GOERING. The Führer did not know about details in concentration camps, about atrocities. In so far as I know him, I do not believe he was informed.

FYFE. I am not asking about details; I am asking about the murder of 4 or 5 million people. Are you suggesting that nobody in power in Germany, except Himmler and perhaps Kaltenbrunner, knew about that?

GOERING. I am still of the opinion that the Führer did not know about these figures.

FYFE. Now, Witness, you said that Hitler, in your opinion, did not know about or was ignorant about the question of concentration camps and the Jews. I would like you to look at document USSR 170.

Now this is a conference which you had with a number of people. Lohse, who was at the conference, says: 'There are only a few Jews left alive, tens of thousands have been disposed of.' Do you still say, in the face of the documents, that neither Hitler nor yourself knew that the Jews were being exterminated?

GOERING. This should be understood. From this you cannot conclude that they have been killed. It is not my remark. The Jews were only left in smaller numbers. From this remark you cannot conclude that they were killed. It could also mean that they were removed.

FYFE. I suggest that you make it clear what is meant by 'there are only a few Jews left alive, whereas tens of thousands have been disposed of'.

GOERING. They were still living there. That is how you should understand that.

FYFE. You heard what I read to you about Hitler. Hitler said the Jews must either work or be shot. That was in April 1943. Do you still say that neither Hitler nor you knew of this policy to exterminate the Jews?

GOERING. For the correction of the document –

FYFE. Will you please answer the question? Do you still say neither Hitler nor you knew of the policy to exterminate the Jews?

GOERING. As far as Hitler is concerned, I have said I do not believe it. As far as I am concerned, I have said that I did not know, even approximately, to what degree this thing took place.

FYFE. You did not know to what degree, but you knew there was a policy that aimed at the extermination of the Jews?

GOERING. No, a policy for emigration, not liquidation, of the Jews. I only knew that there had been isolated cases of such perpetrations.

FYFE. Thank you.

GENERAL RUDENKO (*chief prosecutor for the USSR*). If I understand you, defendant Goering, you said that all the basic decisions concerning foreign, political and military matters were taken by Hitler alone? Do I understand you rightly?

GOERING. Yes, certainly. After all, he was the Führer.

RUDENKO. Am I to understand that Hitler took these decisions without listening to the opinions of the experts who studied the questions, and the intelligence reports on those matters?

GOERING. It depended upon the circumstances. In certain cases, he would ask for data to be submitted to him, without the experts knowing the exact reason.

RUDENKO. 16th September, 1941, is the date of this document. Paragraph B of the document. It states that as a general rule the death of one German soldier must be paid for by the lives of 50 to 100 Communists. I am interested in whether this document was unknown to you.

GOERING. Yes, it was. It was not directed to me either. Here again it merely went to some administrative office. The Air Force had very little to do with such matters.

RUDENKO. Please tell me, do you know about Himmler's directives given in 1941 about the extermination of 30 million Slavs?

GOERING. Yes. This was not an order, but a speech. In all speeches Himmler made to assistant leaders, he insisted on the strictest secrecy.

Consequently, I have no knowledge of this nonsense.

RUDENKO. You did not know about it. Very well. Tell me, in the German totalitarian State was there not a governing centre, which meant Hitler and his immediate entourage, in which you acted as deputy? Could Himmler of his own volition have issued directives for the extermination of 30 million Slavs without being empowered by Hitler or by you?

GOERING. Himmler gave no order for the extermination of 30 million Slavs. Had Himmler issued such an order de facto, then he would have had to ask the Führer, not me, but the Führer, and the latter would probably have told him at once that it was impossible.

RUDENKO. I have a few concluding questions to put to you. First of all, regarding the so-called theory of the Master Race. Were you in accord with this principle of the Master Race and education of the German people in the spirit of it or were you not in accord with it?

GOERING. I have never expressed my agreement with the theory that one race should be considered as a Master Race superior to the others, but I have emphasised the difference between races.

RUDENKO. You can answer this question; apparently you do not consider it right?

GOERING. I personally do not consider it right.

RUDENKO. The next question: You have stated here at the Tribunal that you did not agree with Hitler regarding the question of annexation of Czechoslovakia, the Jewish Question, the question of war with the Soviet Union, the value of the theory of the Master Race, and the question of the shooting of the British airmen who were prisoners of war. How would you explain that, having such serious differences, you still thought it possible to collaborate with Hitler and to carry out his policy?

GOERING. All right. I may have had a different opinion from that of my supreme leader, and I may also express my opinion clearly. If the supreme leader insists on his opinion and I have sworn allegiance to him, then the discussion comes to an end, just as is the case elsewhere. I do not think I need to elaborate that point.

RUDENKO. In other words, you thought it possible, even in spite of these differences, to collaborate with Hitler?

GOERING. I have emphasised it and I maintain that it is true. My oath does not only hold good in good times but also in bad times, although the Führer never threatened me and never told me that he was afraid for my health.

RUDENKO. If you thought it possible to co-operate with Hitler, do you recognise that, as the second man in Germany, you are responsible for the organising on a national scale of murders of millions of innocent people, independently of whether you knew about those facts or not? Tell me briefly: yes or no.

GOERING. No, because I did not know anything about them and did not cause them . . . If I actually did not know them., I cannot be held responsible for them.

RUDENKO. It was your duty to know about these facts.

GOERING. In what way my duty? Either I know the fact, or I do not know it. You can only ask me if I was negligent in failing to obtain knowledge.

RUDENKO. You ought to know yourself better. Millions of Germans knew about the crimes which were being perpetrated, and you did not know about them?

GOERING. Neither did millions of Germans know about them. That is a statement which has in no way been proved.

RUDENKO. You stated to the Tribunal that Hitler's Government brought great prosperity to Germany. Are you still sure that that is so?

GOERING. Definitely until the beginning of the war. The collapse was only due to the war being lost.

RUDENKO. I have no more questions.

PRESIDENT. Dr Stahmer do you wish to re-examine the witness?

DR STAHMER. During your examination, you stated regarding certain accusations, that you want to assume responsibility for them.

GOERING. I acknowledge my responsibility for having done everything to carry out the preparations for the seizure of power, and to have made the power firm in order to make Germany free and great. I did everything to avoid this war. But after it started, it was my duty to do everything to win it.

PRESIDENT. Will you state your full name?

KEITEL (*Chief of the High Command of the Armed Forces*). Wilhelm Keitel.

PRESIDENT. Will you repeat this oath after me: I swear by God the Almighty and Omniscient, that I will speak the pure truth, and will withhold and add nothing.

The witness repeated the oath.

You may sit down if you wish. Dr Nelte do you wish to examine the witness?

DR NELTE. Do you have any sons?

KEITEL. I had three sons, all of whom served at the front as officers during this war. The youngest one died in battle in Russia in 1941. The second was a major in Russia and has been missing in action, and the eldest son, who was a major, is a prisoner of war.

NELTE. Field Marshal Keitel, to begin with essential matters, I would like to put the following basic questions to you:

What basic attitude did you as a soldier, an officer, and a general have toward the problems with which you came into contact in your profession?

KEITEL. I can say that I was a soldier by inclination and conviction. For more than 44 years without interruption I served my country and my people as a soldier, and I tried to do my best in the service of my profession. I did this with the same devotion under the Kaiser, under President Ebert, under Field Marshal von Hindenburg, and under the Führer, Adolf Hitler.

NELTE. What is your attitude today?

KEITEL. As a German officer, I naturally consider it my duty to admit what I have done, even if it should have been wrong. I am grateful that I am being given the opportunity to give an account here and before the German people of what I was and my participation in the events which have taken place. It will not always be possible to differentiate clearly whether it was guilt or circumstances.

I am convinced that the large mass of our brave soldiers were basically decent, and that where even they overstepped the bounds of acceptable behaviour, our soldiers acted in good faith, believing in the military necessity, and the orders which they received.

NELTE. Will you please tell us something about the co-operation between you and Hitler? Much will depend upon discovering in what manner your work with Hitler can be estimated, particularly to what extent you could be considered his collaborator or adviser. Will you tell me whether Hitler discussed his plans with you in the manner which is customary in close collaboration?

KEITEL. In general I must answer no. It was not in any way in keeping with Hitler's peculiar disposition and personality to have advisers of that kind. One had to assist by procuring documents, but concerning the main point, the decision itself, he did not brook any influence. Therefore, strange as it may sound, the final answer always was: 'This is my decision and it is unalterable'. That was the announcement of his decision.

NELTE. I would like to know whether the expression 'intimate' which is contained in the Indictment, is correct in order to describe the relations between you and Hitler, privately or officially?

KEITEL. I found the word 'intimate' in the Indictment and I asked myself the question, 'Where did this conception originate?' To be quite frank, I can only answer that no one ever heard a single word from me about the actual and constant difficulties that I had. I kept quiet about them. Intimate relations are, according to my definition of 'intimate' – I do not know if in the English translation 'intimate' expresses the same thing which we call 'intim' – mean relations where there is confidence and frank discussions and these did not exist. Intimacy was not Hitler's attitude towards the older generals to whose circle I also belonged.

NELTE. I come to the question of re-armament, and the various cases of Austria, Czechoslovakia, etc. I would like to ask you about the accusation of the prosecution, that you participated in the planning and preparation of wars of aggression. Will you tell us your views on that subject?

KEITEL. As a soldier, I must say that the term, war of aggression, as used here is meaningless as far as I am concerned; we learned how to conduct aggressive warfare, defensive actions, and actions of retreat. However, according to my own personal feeling as a military man, the concept 'war of aggression' is a purely political concept and not a military one. I mean that if the Wermacht and the soldier, are a tool of the politicians, they are not qualified in my opinion to decide or to judge whether these military operations did or did not constitute a war of aggression. These decisions are not the task of the soldier, but solely that of the statesman.

NELTE. But you are not only a soldier, you are also an individual with a life of your own. When facts brought to your notice in your professional capacity revealed that a projected operation was unjust, did you not have private and personal doubts?

KEITEL. I believe I can truthfully say that throughout the whole of my military career I was brought up, so to speak, in the old tradition which never concerned itself in this question. Naturally, one has one's opinion and a life of one's own, but in the exercise of professional functions as a soldier and officer this life has been given away, yielded up.

RUDENKO. Defendant Keitel, I am asking you about the directive concerning the so-called Communist insurrectionary movement in the occupied territories. It is dated September 16, 1941. It states: 'One must bear in mind that human life in the countries affected has absolutely no value, and that intimidation is only possible through the application of extraordinarily harsh measures'. You remember this basic idea of the order, that human life is absolutely valueless. Do you remember this statement, the basic statement of the order, that 'human life has absolutely no value'? Do you remember this sentence?

KEITEL. Yes.

RUDENKO. You signed the order containing this statement?

KEITEL. Yes.

RUDENKO. Do you consider that necessity demanded this extremely evil order?

KEITEL. These instructions were addressed in the first place to the Supreme Commander of the Wehrmacht offices in the south-east; that is, in the Balkan regions where extensive partisan guerilla warfare and a war between the leaders had assumed enormous proportions, and, secondly, because the same phenomena had been observed and established on the same or a similar scale in certain defined areas of the occupied Soviet territotory.

THE PRESIDENT. The Tribunal considers that you are not answering the question. The question was perfectly capable of an answer 'yes' or 'no' and an explanation afterwards.

RUDENKO. I ask you once more, do you consider this order, this particular order – and I emphasise – in which it is stated that 'human life has absolutely no value'. Do you consider this order correct?

KEITEL. It does not contain these words, but I knew from years of experience that in the south-eastern territories and in certain parts of the Soviet territory human life was not highly valued.

RUDENKO. You say that these words do not figure in the order?

KEITEL. Those exact words do not appear to my knowledge; but it says that human life has very little value in these territories. I remember something like that.

RUDENKO. These are documents 389-PS and R-98. Defendant Keitel, have you familiarised yourself with the documents?

KEITEL. Yes. The text in the German language says that 'human life in the countries affected frequently has no value'.

RUDENKO. And further?

KEITEL. ' . . . and they can be intimidated by extreme harshness as atonement for the life of a German soldier.'

RUDENKO. Quite clear. And in this same order in this same sub-paragraph 'b' it is stated that: 'To atone for the death of one German soldier, 50 to 100 Communists must, as a rule, be sentenced to death. The method of execution should strengthen the intimidation measure'. Is that correct?

KEITEL. The German text is slightly different. It says: 'Generally speaking, 50 to 100 persons must be sentenced to death in such cases'.

That is the German wording.

RUDENKO. For one German soldier?

KEITEL. Yes. I know that and I see it here.

RUDENKO. That is what I was asking you about. So now I ask you once more . . .

KEITEL. Do you want an explanation of that or am I not to say any more?

RUDENKO. I shall now interrogate you on this matter. I ask you whether, when signing this order, you thereby expressed your personal opinion on these cruel measures? In other words, were you in agreement with Hitler?

KEITEL. I signed the order, but the figures contained in it are alterations made personally in the order by Hitler himself.

RUDENKO. And what figures did you present to Hitler?

KEITEL. The figures in the original were 5 to 10.

RUDENKO. In other words, the divergence between you and Hitler consisted merely in the figures and not in the spirit of the document?

KEITEL. The idea was that the only way of intimidating them was to demand several sacrifices for the life of one soldier, as is stated here.

RUDENKO. But you . . .

THE PRESIDENT. That was not an answer to the question. The question was whether the only difference between you and Hitler on this document was a question of figures. That admits of the answer, Yes or No. Was the only difference between you and Hitler a question of figures?

KEITEL. Then I must say that with reference to the underlying principle there was a difference of opinion, the final results of which I no longer feel myself in a position to justify, since I added my signature on behalf of my department.

RUDENKO. You considered yourself a member of the Nazi Party?

KEITEL. I have always thought of myself as a soldier; not as a political soldier or politician.

RUDENKO. Should we not conclude, after all that has been said here, that you were a 'Hitler' General, not because duty called you but on account of your own convictions?

KEITEL. I have stated here that I was a true and obedient soldier of my Führer. I do not think that there are generals in Russia who do not give Marshal Stalin implicit obedience.

RUDENKO. I have no further questions.

MAXWELL FYFE. Just look at page 110(a) of the document book which you have. This is quite an early order of the 1st of October, 1941:

'Attacks committed lately on members of the armed forces in the occupied territories necessitate emphasising that it is advisable that military commanders always have at their disposal a number of hostages of different political tendencies, namely:

1. Nationalists

2. Democratic-bourgeois, and

3. Communists.

It is important that these should include well-known, leading personalities or members of their families whose names are to be made public. Hostages belonging to the same group as the culprit are to be shot in case of attacks. It is asked that commanders be instructed accordingly. (Signed) Keitel.'

Why were you so particular that, if you happened to arrest a democratic-bourgeois, your commanders should have a sufficient bag of democratic-bourgeois as hostages to shoot? I thought you were not a politician.

KEITEL. I was not at all particular and the idea did not originate with me; but it is in accordance with the instructions – the official regulations – regarding hostages which state that those held as hostages must come from the circles responsible for the attacks.

MAXWELL FYFE. I am asking you a perfectly simple question, defendant. Did you or did you not approve of a number of democratic-bourgeois being taken as hostages for one democratic-bourgeois who happened to be -

KEITEL. It does not say so in the document; it only says that hostages must be taken. It says nothing about shooting them.

MAXWELL FYFE. Would you mind looking at it since you correct me so emphatically – depending upon the membership of the culprits, that is, whether they are nationalists, or democratic-bourgeois or communists, 'hostages of the corresponding group are to be shot in case of attacks'.

KEITEL. If that is in the document then I must have carried it out in that way.

MAXWELL FYFE. Now answer my question. Did you approve of that?

KEITEL. I personally had different views on the hostage system; but I signed it, because I had been ordered to do so.

PRESIDENT. Dr Nelte, do you wish to re-examine?

DR NELTE. How was it possible and how do you explain that orders and instructions were carried out and passed on by you and how is it that no effective resistance was met with?

KEITEL. To find an explanation for this, I must say that you had to know the Führer, that you had to know what atmosphere I worked in day and night for years.

The Führer would advance arguments which to him appeared decisive in his own forceful and convincing way, stating the military and political necessities and making felt his concern for the welfare of his soldiers and their safety as well as his concern about the future of our people.

So I would transmit the orders that were given, and promulgated them without letting myself be deterred by any possible effects they might have.

But never did it enter my mind to revolt against the Head of the State and the Supreme Commander of the Armed Forces or refuse him obedience. As far as I am concerned as a soldier, loyalty is sacred to me. I may be accused of having made mistakes, and also of having shown weakness in face of the Führer, Adolf Hitler. But never can it be said that I was cowardly, dishonourable or faithless.

PRESIDENT. Now Dr Kauffmann.

KAUFFMANN. With the agreement of the tribunal I now call the witness Hoess.

PRESIDENT. Will you state your name.

HOESS. Rudolf Franz Ferdinand Hoess.

THE PRESIDENT. Will you repeat this oath after me: I swear by God, the Almighty and Omniscent, that I will speak the pure truth and will withhold and add nothing?

The witness repeated the oath.

PRESIDENT. Will you sit down?

DR KURT KAUFFMANN (*counsel for Kaltenbrunner*). Witness, your statements will have far-reaching significance. You are perhaps the only one who can throw some light upon certain hidden aspects, and who can tell what people gave the order for the destruction of European Jewry, and can further state how this order was carried out and to what degree the execution was kept a secret.

PRESIDENT. Dr Kauffmann, will you kindly put questions to the witness?

KAUFFMANN. Yes. From 1940 to 1943, you were the commandant of the camp at Auschwitz. Is that true?

HOESS. Yes.

KAUFFMANN. And during that time, hundreds of thousands of human beings were sent to their death there. Is that correct?

HOESS. Yes.

KAUFFMANN. Is it true that you, yourself, have made no exact notes regarding the figures of the number of those victims because you were forbidden to make them?

HOESS. Yes, that is correct.

KAUFFMANN. Is it furthermore correct that only one man, by the name of Eichmann, recorded the figure, the man who had the task of organising and assembling these people?

HOESS. Yes.

KAUFFMANN. Is it furthermore true that Eichmann stated to you that in Auschwitz a sum total of more than 2 million Jews had been destroyed?

HOESS. Yes.

KAUFFMANN. Men, women, and children?

HOESS. Yes.

KAUFFMANN. You were a participant in the (First) World War?

HOESS. Yes.

KAUFFMANN. And then, in 1922, you entered the Party?

HOESS. Yes.

KAUFFMANN. Were you a member of the SS?

HOESS. Since 1934.

KAUFFMANN. And then at the end of 1934, you went to the concentration camp at Dachau?

HOESS. Yes.

KAUFFMANN. When were you commandant at Auschwitz?

HOESS. I was commandant at Auschwitz from May 1940 until 1st December, 1943.

KAUFFMANN. What was the highest number of internees ever held at one time at Auschwitz?

HOESS. The highest number of internees held at one time at Auschwitz was about 140,000 men and women.

KAUFFMANN. Is it true that in 1941, you were ordered to Berlin to see Himmler? Please, state briefly what was discussed.

HOESS. Yes. In the summer of 1941, I was summoned to Berlin to Reichsführer SS Himmler to receive personal orders. He told me something to the effect – I don't remember the exact words – that the Führer had given the order for a definite solution of the Jewish question. We, the SS, must carry out that order. If it was not carried out now then the Jews would later on destroy the German people. We had chosen Auschwitz because of its easy access by rail and also because the extensive site could readily be isolated.

KAUFFMANN. During that conference, did Himmler tell you that this planned action had to be treated as a 'Secret Reich Matter' (*Geheime Reichssache*).

HOESS. Yes. He stressed the point. He told me not to say anything about it to my immediate superior, Gruppenführer Glucks. This conference only concerned the two of us and I was to observe the strictest secrecy.

KAUFFMANN. Does the expression, 'Secret Reich Matter' mean that no one was permitted to make even the slightest allusion to outsiders without endangering his own life?

HOESS. Yes, 'Secret Reich Matter' means that no one was allowed to speak about such matter with any person and that everyone promised upon his life to observe the utmost secrecy.

KAUFFMANN. Did you break that promise?

HOESS. No, not until the end of 1942.

KAUFFMANN. Why did you mention that date? Did you talk to outsiders after that date?

HOESS. At the end of 1942 my wife's curiosity was aroused by remarks made by the then Gauleiter of Upper Silesia regarding happenings in my camp. She asked me whether this was the truth and I admitted that it was. Otherwise, I have never talked about it to anybody else.

KAUFFMANN. Will you briefly tell whether it is correct that the camp at Auschwitz was completely isolated, and describe the measures taken to ensure the secrecy of the carrying out of the task given to you?

HOESS. The camp Auschwitz as such was about 3 kilometres from the town. About 20,000 acres of the surrounding country had been cleared of all inhabitants, and the entire area could only be entered by SS men or civilian employees who had special passes. The actual compound called 'Birkenau', where later on the extermination camp was constructed, was situated 2 kilometres from the Auschwitz camp. The camp installations themselves, that is to say the provisional installations used at first, were deep in the woods and could from nowhere be detected by the eye. In addition to that, this area had been declared a prohibited area and not even members of the SS who did not have a special pass could enter it. Thus it was impossible, as far as one could judge, for anyone, except authorised persons, to enter the area.

KAUFFMANN. Were there any signs that might indicate to an outsider, who saw railway transports arrive, that people were being destroyed or was that possibility so small because there was in Auschwitz an unusually large number of incoming transports consisting of shipments of material and so forth?

HOESS. Yes, an observer who did not make notes exclusively for that purpose could obtain no idea about that . . . The trains themselves were closed, that is to say, the doors of the freight cars were closed so that it was not possible, from the outside, to see the people being transported.

KAUFFMANN. And after the arrival of the transports did the victims have to dispose of everything they had? Did they have to undress completely; did they have to surrender their valuables? Is that true?

HOESS. Yes.

KAUFFMANN. And then they immediately went to their death?

HOESS. Yes.

KAUFFMANN. I ask you, according to your knowledge, did these people know what was in store for them?

HOESS. The majority of them did not, for steps were taken to keep them in doubt about it so that the suspicion would not arise that they were to go to their death. For instance, all doors and all walls bore inscriptions to the effect that they were going to undergo a delousing operation or take a shower. This was proclaimed in several languages to the detainees by other detainees who had come in with earlier transports and who were being used as auxiliary crews during the whole action.

KAUFFMANN. And then, you told me the other day, that death from gassing occurred within a period of 3 to 15 minutes. Is that correct?

HOESS. Yes.

KAUFFMANN. You also told me that even before death definitely set in the victims fell into a state of unconsciousness?

HOESS. Yes. From what I was able to find out myself or from what was told me by medical officers, the time necessary for the arrival of unconsciousness or death varied according to the temperature and the number of people present in the chambers. Loss of consciousness took place after a few seconds or minutes.

KAUFFMANN. Did you yourself ever sympathise with the victims, thinking of your own family and children?

HOESS. Yes.

KAUFFMANN. How was it possible then for you to carry out these actions?

HOESS. In spite of all the doubts which I had, the only one and decisive argument was the strict order and the reason given for it by the SS Reichsführer Himmler.

KAUFFMANN. I ask you whether Himmler inspected the camp and convinced himself that the order for annihilation was being carried out?

HOESS. Yes. Himmler visited the camp in 1942 and he watched in detail one processing from beginning to end.

KAUFFMANN. Does the same apply to Eichmann?

HOESS. Eichmann came repeatedly to Auschwitz and knew precisely what was being done there.

KAUFFMANN. I ask you whether you have any knowledge regarding the treatment of detainees, whether certain methods became known to you according to which detainees were tortured and cruelly treated?

HOESS. The main reason why detainees towards the end of the war were in such bad condition, why so many thousands of them were found sick and emaciated in the camps, was that every detainee had to be employed in the armament industry to the extreme limit of his physical power.

KAUFFMANN. Therefore, there can be no doubt that the longer the war lasted, the larger became the number of the ill-treated and also tortured inmates. Didn't you ever when you inspected the concentration camps learn something of this state of affairs through complaints etc, or do you consider that the conditions which have been described are more or less due to sporadic excesses of individual officials?

HOESS. These so-called ill-treatments and torturing in concentration camps, stories of which were spread everywhere amongst the people, and particularly by detainees who were liberated by the occupying armies were not, as assumed, inflicted methodically, but by individual leaders, sub-leaders and men who laid violent hands on them.

KAUFFMANN. To what do you attribute the particularly bad and shameful conditions which were found on invasion by allied troops, and which to an extent were photographed and filmed?

HOESS. The catastrophic situation at the end of the war was due to the fact that as a result of the destruction of the railways and of the continuous bombing of the industrial works, it was no longer possible to properly care for these masses, for example Auschwitz with its 140,000 detainees.

DR THOMA (*Rosenberg's counsel*). Herr Rosenberg, please give the Tribunal your biographical data.

ROSENBERG. I was born on 12th January 1893, in Revel, Estonia. When the German-Russian front lines approached in 1915, the Institute of Technology was evacuated to Moscow and there I continued my studies. To the Baltic Germans, notwithstanding their loyalty toward the Russian State, the Homeland of German culture was their intellectual home and the experience I had in Russia strengthened my decision to do everything within my power to help to prevent the political movement in Germany from backsliding into Bolshevism.

THOMA. You mentioned Germany as your intellectual home. Will you tell the Tribunal through which studies and by which scientists you were influenced in favour of Germany?

ROSENBERG. In addition to my immediate interest in architecture and painting, I had since childhood pursued historical and philosophical studies and thus, of course, I felt compelled to read Goethe, Herder and Fichte in order to develop intellectually along these lines. At the same, I was influenced by the social ideas of Charles Dickens, Carlyle and Emerson.

THE PRESIDENT. The Tribunal wants you to confine yourself to your own philosophy and not to the origins of these philosophies, in so far as you are referring to philosophical subjects at all.

THOMA. How did you come to the National Socialist party and to Hitler in Munich?

ROSENBERG. In May 1919, the publisher of a journal was visited by a man by the name of Anton Drexler, who introduced himself as the chairman of the newly founded German Labour Party. There, in the autumn of 1919, I also met Hitler.

THOMA. When did you join Hitler?

ROSENBERG. Well, at the time I had a serious conversation with Hitler, and on that occasion I noticed his broad view of the entire European situation. He said that, in his opinion, Europe was at that time going through a social and political crisis.

I would like to add that the name 'National Socialism', I believe, originated in the Sudetenland, and there the small German Labour Party was founded under the name of 'National Socialist German Labour Party'. We considered that the representation of national interests should not be based on privileges of certain classes but, on the contrary, on a national basis; the demand for national unity and dignified representation on the part of the people was the right attitude. This resulted for Hitler in the device . . .

THE PRESIDENT (*interposing*). Dr Thoma, would you try to confine the witness to the charges which are against him?

THOMA. In my opinion, we have to devote some time to Rosenberg's train of thought to determine the motives for his actions, but I will now ask him this:

Why did you fight against democracy, as a matter of international struggle?

MR DODD (*executive trial counsel*). Mr President, I should like to say that no one in the prosecution has made any charge against this defendant for what he has thought. I think we are all, as a matter of principle, opposed to prosecuting any man for what he thinks.

THOMA. To my knowledge, the defendant is also accused of fighting democracy, and that is why I believe I should put this question to him.

THE PRESIDENT. What is the question?

THOMA. Why he was fighting democracy, why National Socialism and he himself fought democracy.

THE PRESIDENT. I don't think that has got anything to with this case. The only question is whether he used National Socialism for the purpose of conducting international offences.

THOMA. To my knowledge, the charge of waging a war of aggression was preferred because it was a war against democracy based on nationalism and militarism.

PRESIDENT (*interposing*). Democracy outside Germany, not in Germany.

THOMA. Then, I would like to ask the defendant how he will answer the charge that National Socialism preached a master-race.

ROSENBERG. I have never heard the word master-race (*Herrenrasse*) as often as in this court-room. To my knowledge I did not mention or use it at all in my writing. I spoke of a master-race as mentioned by Homer only once, and I found a quotation from a British author who, in writing about the life of Lord Kitchener, said the Englishman who had conquered the world had proved himself as a creative superman (*Herrenmensch*).

THOMA. Now, I would like to ask the following question: you believed that the so-called Jewish problem in Europe could only be solved by removing the Jews from the European

continent. How and why did you arrive at that opinion?
I mean to say, how in your opinion would the departure of
the last Jew from Europe solve the problem?

ROSENBERG. It seemed to me that after an epoch of generous
emancipation in the course of national movements of the
nineteenth century, an essential part of the Jewish nation
also remembered its own tradition and its own character and
more and more consciously segregated itself from other
nations.

But my attitude in the political sphere to the Jewish question
was due partly to my observations and experience of Jews
in Russia and later to my experience of them in Germany,
which especially seemed to confirm their strangeness.

THOMA. Herr Rosenberg, what do you have to say to the fact
that in the First World War 12,000 Jewish soldiers died at
the front?

ROSENBERG. Of course, I was always conscious of the fact
that many Jewish-German citizens were assimilated into the
German environment. But on the whole this did not involve
the entire social and political movement . . . Prominent
Jewish people and the chairman of the Democratic party
suggested three times quite openly that in view of the
increase in unemployment Germans should be deported to
Africa and Asia.

THOMA. Herr Rosenberg, you were the official appointed by
the Führer for the supervision of the entire Spiritual and
Ideological Education of the National Socialist party. Did
you exert any influence on national law-making in that
capacity?

ROSENBERG. The Party Chancellery occasionally asked me
to define my position with regard to this or that question but
was not obliged to take my views into consideration.

THOMA. Witness, did you know anything about concentration
camps?

ROSENBERG. Yes. this question, of course, has been put to
everybody, and the fact that concentration camps existed
became known to me in 1933. But I must state that I knew

by name only two concentration camps, Kranienburg and Dachau.

THOMA. Did you participate in the evacuation of Jews from Germany?

ROSENBERG. I should perhaps add one thing; I visited no real concentration camp, neither Dachau nor any other one. I once questioned Himmler – it was in 1938 – about the concentration camps and told him that one saw in the foreign Press all sorts of reports of alleged atrocities which were being committed in them. Himmler said to me: 'Why don't you come to Dachau and take a look at things for yourself? We have a swimming pool there, we have sanitary installations – irreproachable – no objections can be raised.'

I did not visit the camp because if something improper had been going on, Himmler would probably not have shown it to me. On the other hand, for reasons of good taste I did not want to go simply to observe people who had been deprived of their liberty.

An American chaplain has very kindly given me in my cell a church paper from Colombus. I gather from that the United States, too, arrested Jehovah's Witnesses during the war and that until December 1945, 11,000 of them were still detained in camps.

I presume that under such conditions, every state would take similar actions against nationals who refused to do war service in some form or another; and that was my attitude too; I could not consider Himmler wrong in this connection.

DODD. Yesterday, you stated before the Tribunal that you did have a discussion with Heinrich Himmler, the SS Reichs-führer, about concentration camps, and if I remember correctly, you said that that was some time in 1938; is that so?

ROSENBERG. Yes. I testified that I discussed the concentration camps with him once, but I cannot say with certainty that it was in 1938, as I did not make a note of it.

DODD. Very good. He suggested you should go through one or the other of these camps, Dachau or some other camp; is that so?

ROSENBERG. Yes, he then told me that I should take a look at the Dachau camp.

DODD. And you declined the invitation?

ROSENBERG. Right.

DODD. And if I recollect correctly, I understood you to say that you declined because you were quite sure that he would not show you the unfavourable things that were in that camp?

ROSENBERG. Yes, I assumed more or less that if there really were unfavourable things, I certainly would not see them anyway.

DODD. You mean that you simply assumed that there were unfavourable things; that you didn't know there were unfavourable things?

ROSENBERG. I heard this through the foreign Press and it is about . . .

DODD. When did you first hear that through the foreign Press?

ROSENBERG. That was in the first months of 1933.

DODD. And did you continuously read the foreign Press about the concentration camps in Germany from 1933 to 1938?

ROSENBERG. I did not read the foreign Press at all for unfortunately I do not speak English. I only received some excerpts from it from time to time, and in the German Press there were occasional references to the allegations in the foreign Press, and it was emphatically denied that there was any truth in these allegations. I can still remember a statement by Goering in which he said that it was beyond his comprehension that anything like that could be written.

DODD. Did you ever talk about the extermination of the Jews?

ROSENBERG. I have not in general spoken about the extermination of the Jews in the sense of this term. One has to consider the words. The term 'extermination' has been used by the British Prime Minister . . .

DODD. You will refer to the words. You just tell me now whether you ever said it or not? You said that you did not?

ROSENBERG. Not in a single speech in that sense.

DODD. I understand the sense. Did you ever talk about it with anybody as a matter of State policy or Party policy, about the extermination of the Jews?

ROSENBERG. In a conference with the Führer there was once an open discussion on this question apropos of an intended speech which was not delivered.

DODD. When was it you were going to deliver that speech? Approximately what was the date?

ROSENBERG. In December, 1941.

DODD. Then you had written into your speech remarks about the extermination of Jews, hadn't you? Answer that yes or no.

ROSENBERG. I have said already that that word does not have the sense which you attribute to it.

DODD. I will come to the word and the meaning of it. I am asking you, did you use the word or the term, extermination of the Jews in the speech which you prepared to make in the Sportpalast in December of 1941? Now, you can answer that pretty simply.

ROSENBERG. That may be, but I do not remember. I myself did not prepare the phrasing of the draft. In which form it was expressed I can no longer say.

DODD. Well then, perhaps we can help you on that. I will ask you be shown Document 1517-PS. It becomes Exhibit USA-824.

Witness handed document.

Now this is a memorandum of yours written by you about a discussion you had with Hitler on 14 December 1941 . . . If you will look at the second paragraph, you will find these words:

'I took the standpoint not to speak of the extermination (*Ausrottung*) of the Jews. The Führer affirmed this and said that they had thrust the war upon us and that they had brought the destruction; it is no wonder if the results would strike them first'.

Now you have indicated that you have some difficulty with the meaning of that word and I am going to ask you about the word, '*Ausrottung*'. I am going to ask you be shown – you are familiar with the Standard German-English dictionary, Cassell's, I suppose, are you? Do you know this work, ever heard of it?

ROSENBERG. No.

DODD. This is something you will be interested in. Will you look up and read out to the Tribunal what the definition of '*Ausrottung*' is?

ROSENBERG. I do not need a foreign dictionary in order to explain what various meanings in the German language the word '*Ausrottung*' may have. One can exterminate an idea, an economic system, a social order and, as a final consequence, also a group of human beings, certainly. Those are many possibilities which are contained in that word. For that I do not need an English-German dictionary. Translations from German into English are so often wrong. For example, in that last document you have submitted to me, I heard again the translation of '*Herrenrasse*'.

DODD. Alright, I am not interested in that. Let us deal on this term of '*Ausrottung*'. I take it then that you agree it does mean to wipe out or to kill off, as it is understood, and that you did use the term in speaking to Hitler.

ROSENBERG. Here again, I hear a different translation, which again used new German words, so I cannot determine what you wanted to express in English.

DODD. Are you very serious in pressing this apparent inability of yours to agree with me about this word or are you trying to kill time? Don't you know that there are plenty of people in this court room who speak German and who agree that that word does mean to wipe out, to extirpate?

ROSENBERG. It means to overcome in one sense and then it is to be used not with respect to individuals but rather to judicial entities, to certain historical traditions. In another sense, the word has been used with respect to the German people and we have not believed that it meant that 60 millions of Germans would be shot.

DODD. I want to remind you that this speech of yours in which you use the term *'Ausrottung'* was about six months after Himmler told Hoess, whom you heard on this witness stand, to start exterminating Jews. That is a fact, is it not?

ROSENBERG. Then, may I perhaps say something about the use of of the words here? We are speaking here of extermination of Jewry; there is also still a difference between Jewry and individual Jews.

DR HANS FLAECHSNER (*Speer's counsel*). Herr Speer, will you please tell the Tribunal about your life up until the time you were appointed minister?

SPEER. I was born on 19th March, 1905. My grandfather and my father were successful architects. At first I wanted to study mathematics and physics but studied architecture, more because of tradition than inclination. In 1934 Hitler noticed me for the first time. Hitler was quite fanatical on the subject of architecture and I received many important constructional contracts from him.

FLAESCHNER. How did your activity as a minister start?

SPEER. In 1942, my predecessor was killed in an aeroplane crash . . . Immediately upon assuming office, it was plain that not building but armament production was to be my main task.

FLAECHSNER. The prosecution makes the charge that you shared the responsibility for the recruitment of foreign workers and prisoners of war and took manpower from concentration camps. What do you say to this?

SPEER. In this connection, neither I nor the ministry were responsible for this. The ministry was a new establishment, which had a technical problem to deal with. It took no competence in any field away from an existing authority.

FLAECHSNER. Herr Speer, in the year 1943, you visited the concentration camp at Mauthausen?

SPEER. The camp, or the small part of the camp which I saw, appeared to me to be very clean. But I did not see any of the workers, any of the camp inmates, since at that time they were all engaged in work.

FLAECHSNER. Did you learn, on your visit to Mauthausen or on another occasion, about the cruelties which took place at this concentration camp and at other concentration camps?

SPEER. No.

FLAECHSNER. Herr Speer, according to this document – Document RF 24, Exhibit USA 179 – you proposed that factories should be staffed entirely with internees from concentration camps. Did you carry that out?

SPEER. No.

FLAECHSNER. As far as you remember, did you ever make statements regarding ideology, anti-Semitism, etc?

SPEER. No, I assume that otherwise the prosecution would be in a position to produce some evidence of such statements.

FLAECHSNER. Were you able to carry on political discussions with Hitler?

SPEER. No, he regarded me as a purely technical Minister. Attempts to discuss political or personal problems with him always failed because of the fact that he was unapproachable. Hitler knew how to confine every man to his own speciality. He himself was therefore the only co-ordinating factor. This was far beyond his strength and also his capacity.

FLAECHSNER. Then, as an expert Minister, do you wish to limit your responsibility to your sphere of work?

SPEER. No, I should like to say something of fundamental importance here. This war has brought inconceivable catastrophe to the German people and has started a world catastrophe. Therefore, it is my unquestionable duty to assume my share of responsibility for this misfortune before the German people . . . In so far as Hitler gave me orders and I carried them out, I assume the responsibility for them. I did not, of course, carry out all the orders which he gave me.

FLAECHSNER. In January, 1945, Speer sent a memorandum to Hitler: 'The material superiority of the enemy can no longer be counter-balanced, even by the bravery of our soldiers'. Herr Speer, what did you mean by the sentence I quoted?

SPEER. During this period, Hitler attributed the outcome of the war in an increasing degree to the failure of the German people: but he never blamed himself.

FLAECHSNER. Was no unified action taken by some of Hitler's closer advisers in this hopeless situation to demand the termination of war?

SPEER. No. No unified action was taken by the leading men in Hitler's circle. A step like this was quite impossible, for these men considered themselves either as pure specialists, or else as people whose job it was to receive orders, or merely resigned themselves to the situation.

FLAECHSNER. You have described how much you did to preserve industrial plants and other economic installations. Did you also act on behalf of the foreign workers?

SPEER. My responsibility was the industrial sector. I felt it my duty, therefore, to hand over my sector undamaged. As regards the foreign workers in Germany, several of my actions were in their favour . . . for example, through the steps which I had taken to secure the food situation.

FLAECHSNER. Herr Speer, during the last phase of the war you were opposed to Hitler and his policies. Why did you not resign?

SPEER. I thought it was my duty to remain at my post.

FLAECHSNER. I have one last question. Was it possible for you to reconcile your actions during the last phase of the war with your oath and your conception of loyalty to Adolf Hitler?

SPEER. There is one loyalty which everyone must always keep and that is loyalty towards one's own people. That duty comes before everything. If I am in a leading position and if I see that acts are being committed against the interests of the nation, I must oppose them. That Hitler had broken faith with the nation must have been clear to every intelligent member of his circle, certainly at the latest in January or February, 1945. Hitler had been given his mission by the people; but he had no right to gamble away the destiny of the people with his own. Therefore, I fulfilled my natural duty as a German. I did not succeed in every way, but I am proud today that with my achievements I was able to render one more service to the workers in Germany and the Occupied Territories.

MR JUSTICE JACKSON. It was known throughout Germany was it not, that the concentration camps were pretty rough places in which to be put?

SPEER. Yes, but not to the extent which has been revealed during this trial.

JACKSON. And the bad reputation of the concentration camps, as a matter of fact, was useful in making people afraid of being sent there, was it not?

SPEER. No doubt concentration camps were a means, a menace used to keep order.

JACKSON. And to keep people at work?

SPEER. I would not like to put it that way. I would say that a great number of the foreign workers in our country did their work quite voluntarily once they had come to Germany.

JACKSON. You knew the policy of the Nazi Party and the policy of the Government towards the Jews, did you not?

SPEER. I knew that the National Socialist policy was anti-Semitic, and I knew that the Jews were being evacuated from Germany.

JACKSON. In fact, you participated in that evacuation, did you not?

SPEER. No . . . It is clear that if the Jews who were evacuated had been allowed to work for me, it would have been a considerable advantage to me.

JACKSON. As I understand it, you knew about the deportation of 100,000 Jews from Hungary for subterranean aeroplane factories and that you made no objection to it. That is true, is it not?

SPEER. That is true, yes.

JACKSON. And whether legal or illegal means were used to obtain workers did not worry you?

SPEER. I consider that in the light of the whole war situation and of our views in general on this question it was justified.

JACKSON. Yes, it was in accordance with the policy of the Government, and that satisfied you at the time, did it not?

SPEER. Yes. I am of the opinion that at the time I took over my office, in February 1942, all the violations of International Law, which later . . . which are now brought up against me, had already been committed.

JACKSON. Later, where you differed with the people who wanted to continue the war to the bitter end, was that you wanted to see Germany have a chance to restore her life. Is that not a fact? Whereas Hitler took the position that, if he could not survive, he did not care whether Germany survived or not?

SPEER. That is true . . . The letter which I wrote to Hitler on the 29th of March, 1945, shows that he said so himself.

The unreasonable people who were still left only amounted perhaps to a few dozens. The remaining 80 millions were perfectly sensible as soon as they knew what the situation really was.

JACKSON. Perhaps you had a sense of responsibility for having put the 80 millions completely in the power of the Führer principle. Did that occur to you, or does it now as you look back on it?

SPEER. May I have the question repeated, because I didn't understand its sense.

JACKSON. You have 80 million sane and sensible people facing destruction; you have a dozen people driving them on to destruction and they, the 80 million, are unable to stop it. And I ask if you have a feeling of responsibility for having established the Führer principle, which Goering has so well described to us, in Germany?

SPEER. I, personally, when I became minister in February, 1942, placed myself at the disposal of the Führer principle. But I admit that in my organisation I soon saw that the Führer principle was in many ways defective and so I tried to weaken its effect. The tremendous danger of the totalitarian system, however, only became really clear at the moment when we were approaching the end. It was then that one could see what the principle really meant, namely, that every order should be carried out without criticism. The combination of Hitler and this system has brought about these tremendous catastrophes in the world.

JACKSON. I want to ask you some questions about your efforts to produce essential goods, and the conditions that this regime was imposing upon labour. I think you can give some information about this. You were frequently at the Krupp plant, were you not?

SPEER. I was at the Krupp plant five or six times.

JACKSON. Very well. I will ask to have you shown Document 230-D which is an inter-office record of the steel switches, and the steel switches which have been found in the camp will be shown to you, 80 of them, distributed according to the reports.

SPEER. Those are nothing but replacements for rubber truncheons. We had no rubber; and, for that reason, the guards probably had something like this. (*Indicating.*)

JACKSON. That is the same inference that I drew from the document.

SPEER. Yes, but the guards did not immediately use these steel switches any more than your police use their rubber truncheons. But they had to have something in their hands. It is the same thing, all over the world.

JACKSON. In a statement some time ago, you said you had a certain responsibility as a minister of the Government for the condition of foreign and German workers . . . You refer to common responsibility. What do you mean by your common responsibility, along with others?

SPEER. Oh, yes. In my opinion, a State functionary has two types of responsibility. One is the responsibility for his own sector and for that, of course, he is fully responsible. But above that, I think that in decisive matters there is and must be, among the leaders, a joint responsibility, for who is to take responsibility for general developments if not the close associates of the Head of State?

PRESIDENT. Dr Flaechsner would you like to re-examine the witness?

FLAECHSNER. Herr Speer, I refer to the answer which you gave to Justice Jackson at the end of the cross-examination, and to clarify that answer I would like to ask you this: in assuming a common responsibility, did you want to acknowledge measurable guilt or co-responsibility under the penal law, or did you want to record an historical responsibility before your own people?

SPEER. That question is very difficult to answer; it is actually one which the Tribunal will decide in its verdict. I only wanted to say that even in an authoritarian system the leaders must accept a common, united responsibility, and that it is impossible after the catastrophe to avoid this responsibility. If the war had been won, the leaders would presumably have laid claim to full responsibility. But to what extent that is punishable or immoral, that I cannot decide and it is not for me to decide.

FRANCIS BIDDLE (*US tribunal member*). You said the concentration camps had a bad reputation, remember? Is that right?

SPEER. Yes.

BIDDLE. What did you mean by 'bad reputation'? What sort of reputation, for what?

SPEER. That is hard to define. It was known in Germany that a stay in a concentration camp was an unpleasant experience. I knew that, but I did not know any details.

BIDDLE. Well, even if you did not know any details, is not 'unpleasant' putting it a little mildly? Wasn't the reputation that violence and physical punishment were used in the camps? Was not that the reputation that you meant? Is not it fair to say that, really?

SPEER. No, that is going a little too far, on the basis of what we knew. I assumed that there was ill-treatment in individual cases, but I did not assume that it was the rule. I did not know that . . . I must explain that during the time I was a Minister, strange as it may sound, I became less disturbed about the fate of concentration camp inmates than I had been before I became a Minister, because while I was in office I heard only good and reassuring reports about the concentration camps from official sources. It was said that the food was being improved, and so on and so forth . . .

Closing speech of ROBERT JACKSON.

JACKSON. It is common to think of our own time as standing at the apex of civilisation, from which the deficiencies of preceding ages may patronisingly be viewed in the light of what is assumed to be 'progress'. The reality is that in the long perspective of history the present century will not hold an admirable position, unless its second half is to redeem its first. No half-century ever witnessed slaughter on such a scale, such cruelties and inhumanities, such wholesale deportations of people into slavery, such annihilations of minorities.

Crimes in the conduct of warfare were planned with thoroughness as a means of ensuring the victory of German arms. I admit that Hitler was the chief villain. But for the defendants to put all blame on him is neither manly nor true. We know that even the head of a State has the same limits to his senses and to the hours of his day as have lesser men. He must rely on others to be his eyes and ears for most that goes on in a great empire. Other legs must run his errands; other hands must execute his plans.

On whom did Hitler rely for such things more than upon these men in the dock? Who led him to believe he had an invincible air armada if not Goering? Who fed his illusion of German invincibility if not Keitel? Who kept his hatred of the Jew inflamed more than Rosenberg?

These men had access to Hitler. They were the Praetorian Guard, and while they were under Caesar's orders, Caesar was always in their hands.

These defendants now ask this Tribunal to say that they are not guilty of planning, executing, or conspiring to commit this long list of crimes and wrongs.

They stand before the record of this trial as bloodstained Gloucester stood by the body of his slain king. He begged of his widow, as they beg of you: 'Say I slew them not'. And the Queen replied: 'Then say they were not slain. But dead they are . . . '. If you were to say of these men that they are not guilty, it would be as true to say there has been no war, there are no slain, there has been no crime.

PRESIDENT. I call upon the Chief Prosecutor for the United Kingdom and Northern Ireland.

Closing speech by SHAWCROSS.

SIR HARTLEY SHAWCROSS. That these defendants participated in and are morally guilty of crimes so frightful that the imagination staggers and reels back at their very contemplation is not in doubt.

In their graves, crying out not for vengeance but that this shall not happen again, 10 million who might be living in peace and happiness at this hour, soldiers, sailors, airmen and civilians killed in battles that ought never to have been.

Nor was that the only or the greatest crime. Not in battle, not in passion, but in the cold, calculated, deliberate attempt to destroy nations and races, to disintegrate the traditions, the institutions and the very existence of free and ancient States.

Two-thirds of the Jews in Europe exterminated, more than 6 million of them on the killers' own figures.

For such crimes these men might well have been proceeded against by summary executive action, and had the treatment, which they had been parties to meting out against so many millions of innocent people been meted out to them, they could hardly have complained. But this Tribunal is to adjudge their guilt not on any moral or ethical basis alone, but according to law.

Let them now, accused murderers as they are, attempt to be-little the power and influence they exercised how they will, we have only to recall their ranting, as they strutted across the stage of Europe dressed in their brief authority, to see the part they played. They did not then tell the German people or the world that they were merely the ignorant, powerless puppets of their Führer. The defendant Speer has said:

'Even in a totalitarian system there must be total responsibility . . . it is impossible after the catastrophe to evade this total responsibility. If the war had been won, the leaders would also have assumed total responsibility.'

Almost immediately after the war had started the organised extermination of the Jewish race began. Hoess describes the improvements that he made at Auschwitz.

He introduced the new gas, Cyclone B, which 'took from three to fifteen minutes to kill the people in the death chamber, dependent on climatic conditions. We knew the people were dead because their screaming stopped . . . '

Let the engineer Graebe speak of the massacre at Dubno:

'On 5th October 1942, my foreman told me that Jews from Dubno had been shot in 3 large pits, each about 30 metres long and 3 metres deep. About 1,500 persons had been killed daily. All of the 5,000 Jews who had been living in Dubno before the pogrom were to be liquidated.

I drove to the site and went directly to the pits. The people who had got off the trucks – men, women, and children of all ages – had to undress upon the orders of an SS man, who carried a riding or dog whip.

They had to put down their clothes in fixed places, sorted according to shoes, top clothing and underclothing. I saw a heap of shoes of about 800 to 1,000 pairs, great piles of underlinen and clothing. Without screaming or weeping these people undressed, stood around in family groups, kissed each other, said farewells, and waited for a sign from another SS man, who stood near the pit, also with a whip in his hand.

During the 15 minutes that I stood near I heard no complaint or plea for mercy. I watched a family of about 8 persons, a man and a woman both about 50 with their children of about 1, 8 and 10, and two grown-up daughters of about 20 to 24.

An old woman with snow-white hair was holding the one-year-old child in her arms and singing to it and tickling it. The child was cooing with delight. The couple were looking on with tears in their eyes.

The father was holding the hand of a boy about 10 years old and speaking to him softly; the boy was fighting his tears. The father pointed to the sky, stroked his head and seemed to explain something to him.

At that moment the SS man at the pit shouted something to his comrade. The latter counted off about 20 persons and instructed them to go behind the earth mound. Among them was the family which I have mentioned.

I well remember a girl, slim and with black hair who, as she passed close to me, pointed to herself and said, "Twenty-three". I walked around the mound and found myself confronted by a tremendous grave. People were closely wedged together and lying on top of each other so that only their heads were visible. Nearly all had blood running over their shoulders from their heads. Some of the people shot were still moving. Some were lifting their arms and turning their heads to show that they were still alive. The pit was already two-thirds full. I estimated that it already contained about 1,000 people.

I looked for the man who did the shooting. He was an SS man, who sat at the edge of the narrow end of the pit, his feet dangling into the pit. He had a tommy gun on his knees and was smoking a cigarette.

The people, completely naked, went down some steps which were cut in the clay wall of the pit and clambered over the heads of the people lying there, to the place to which the SS man directed them. They laid down in front of the dead or injured people; some caressed those who were still alive and spoke to them in a low voice. Then I heard a series of shots. I looked into the pit and saw that the bodies were twitching or the heads lying motionless on top of the bodies which lay before them. Blood was running away from ther necks.

I was surprised I was not ordered away . . . On the morning of the next day, when I again visited the site, I saw about 30 naked people lying near the pit – about 30 to 50 metres away from it. Some of them were still alive; they looked straight in front of them with a fixed stare and seemed to notice neither the chilliness of the morning nor the workers of my firm who stood around. A girl of about 20 spoke to me and asked me to give her clothes and help her escape. At that moment we heard a fast car approach and I noticed that it was an SS detail. I moved away to my site. Ten minutes later we heard shots from the vicinity of the pit. The Jews still alive had been ordered to throw the corpses into the pit; then they had themselves to lie down in this to be shot in the neck.'

The proposition you are asked to accept is that a man who was either a minister or a leading executive in a State which, within the space of 6 years, transported in horrible conditions some 7 million men, women, and children for labour, exterminated 275,000 of its own aged and mentally infirm, and annihilated in gas chambers or by shooting what must at the lowest computation be 12 million people, remained ignorant or or irresponsible for these crimes.

You are asked to accept that the horrors of the transports, of the conditions of this slave labour, deployed as it was in labour camps throughout the country, the smell of the burning bodies, all of which were known to the world, were not known to these 21 men, by whose orders such things were done.

In one way the fate of these men means little; their personal power for evil lies for ever broken; they have convicted and discredited each other and finally destroyed the legend they created round the figure of their leader.

This trial must form a milestone in the history of civilisation, not only bringing retribution to these guilty men, but also that the ordinary people of the world (and I make no distinction between friend or foe) are now determined that the individual must transcend the State.

You will remember when you come to give your decision the story of Dubno, but not in vengeance – in a determination that these things shall not occur again.

'The father' – do you remember – 'pointed to the sky, and seemed to say something to his boy.'

THE PRESIDENT. Article 24 (j) provides that each defendant may make a statement to the Tribunal. I therefore now call upon the defendants who wish – whether they wish to make statements. Defendant Hermann Wilhelm Goering.

GOERING. The prosecution uses the fact that I was the second man of the State as proof that I must have known everything that happened. But it does not present any documentary or other convincing proof in cases where I have denied under oath that I knew about certain things, or even desired them.

Repeatedly we have heard here how the worst crimes were veiled with the utmost secrecy. I wish to state expressly that I condemn utterly these terrible mass murders and so that there shall be no misunderstanding in this connection, I wish to state emphatically and quite clearly once more before the High Tribunal that I have never decreed the murder of a single individual at any time nor decreed any other atrocities nor tolerated them, while I had the power and the knowledge to prevent them.

I stand behind the things that I have done, but I deny most emphatically that my actions were dictated by the desire to subjugate foreign peoples, or to commit atrocities or crimes. The only motive which guided me was my ardent love for my people, and my desire for their happiness and freedom. And for this I call on the Almighty and my German people as witness.

THE PRESIDENT. I call on the defendant Wilhelm Keitel.

KEITEL. It is far from my intention to minimise my part in what took place. At the end of this Trial, I want to present frankly the avowal and confession I have to make today. In the course of the Trial my defence counsel submitted two fundamental questions to me:

'In case of victory would you have refused to participate in any part of the success?' I answered: 'No, I should certainly have been proud of it'.

The second question was : 'How would you act if you were in the same position again?' My answer: 'Then I would rather choose death than allow myself to be drawn into the net of such pernicious methods'.

I believed, I erred, and I was not in a position to prevent what should have been prevented. That is my guilt.

It is tragic to have to realise that the best I had to give as a soldier, obedience and loyalty, was exploited for purposes which could not be recognised at the time, and that I did not see that there is a limit set even for a soldier's performance of his duty. That is my fate.

THE PRESIDENT. I call on the defendant Alfred Rosenberg.

ROSENBERG. Besides repeating the old accusations, the prosecution claims that we all attended secret conferences in order to plan a war of aggression. Besides that, we are supposed to have ordered the alleged murder of 12 million people. These accusations are described as 'genocide' – the murder of peoples. In this connection, I wish to summarise as follows. I know my conscience to be completely free from any such guilt. I attempted to improve the physical and spiritual conditions of their existence; instead of destroying their personal security and human dignity.

The thought of a physical annihilation of Slavs and Jews, that is to say the actual murder of entire peoples, has never entered my mind. I was of the opinion that the existing Jewish question would have to be solved by the creation of a minority right, emigration, or by settling Jews in a national territory. The White Paper of the British Government of 24th July, 1946, shows how historical developments can bring about measures which were never previously planned.

I understood my struggle, just as it was understood by many thousands of my comrades, to be one conducted for the noblest idea, an idea which had been fought for under flying banners for over a hundred years.

THE PRESIDENT. I call on the defendant Albert Speer.

SPEER. Mr President, may it please the Tribunal: Hitler and the collapse of his system have brought a time of tremendous suffering upon the German people. The useless continuation of the war and the unnecessary destruction make the work of reconstruction more difficult. Privation and misery have come to the German people. After this trial, the German people will despise and condemn Hitler as the proved author of its misfortune. But the world will learn from these happenings not only to hate dictatorship as a form of government, but to fear it.

Hitler's dictatorship differed in one fundamental point from all its predecessors in history. His was the first dictatorship in the present period of modern technical development, a dictatorship which made a complete use of all technical means in a perfect manner for the domination of its own country.

Through technical devices like the radio and the loudspeaker, 80 million people were deprived of independent thought. It was thereby possible to subject them to the will of one man. The telephone, teletype and radio made it possible, for instance, that orders from the highest sources could be transmitted directly to the lowest ranking units by whom, because of the high authority, they were carried out without criticism. Therefore, the more technical the world becomes, the more necessary is the promotion of individual freedom and the individual's awareness of himself as a counterbalance.

In 5 to 10 years, the technique of warfare will make it possible to fire rockets from continent to continent with uncanny precision. By atomic fission it can destroy one million people in the centre of New York in a matter of seconds. Science is able to spread pestilence among human beings and animals and to destroy crops by insect warfare. Chemistry has developed terrible weapons with which it can inflict unspeakable suffering upon helpless human beings.

This Trial must contribute towards preventing such degenerate wars in the future and towards establishing rules whereby human beings can live together.

Of what importance is my own fate after everything that has happened in comparison with this high goal?

It is not war alone which shapes the history of humanity, but also, in a higher sense, the cultural achievements which one day will become the common property of all humanity. But a nation which believes in its future will never perish. May God protect Germany and the culture of the West.

Sir Hartley Shawcross: After Nuremberg . . .

We have since failed to establish a tribunal to deal with such crimes if they occur. This could have been done long ago either by establishing an International Court of Criminal Justice akin to the existing Court of International Justice at The Hague, or by giving a criminal jurisdiction to that court. So far – although I have tried to persuade the UK Government and others – the international community has failed to agree on such a policy. And here I refer not to the United Nations as an institution but to its individual member states. For the Assembly of the UN did indeed on my motion in 1948 vote in favour of such a tribunal. At the time of the Gulf War, much lip service was given to International Law. I cannot help feeling, however, that law or no law, the United States and ourselves would have felt compelled by our political and economic interests in the Middle East to go to the assistance of Kuwait.

What is particularly to be regretted is that Saddam Hussein's surrender for trial by an international tribunal was not insisted upon as a term of the armistice with Iraq. And that no effort has since been made to set up a permanent International Criminal Jurisdiction. Mrs Thatcher had at an early stage expressly stated that Saddam Hussein would be brought to trial 'as the Nazi leaders were at Nuremberg'. But when the armistice became possible the Americans were so anxious to get 'their boys' back home that they did not make the further two days' march to Baghdad, with the result that Saddam saved a large part of his crack regiment and still holds fast to the leadership. Since the end of the Gulf War I have made several public statements urging the establishment of an international court and have written more than once to the Prime Minister – only to receive charming but wholly non-committal replies. International law will never gain its full impact until an international court is established. Nor would the establishment

of such a court present any great difficulty whether financially
or politically.

From 'Nuremberg and the Nazi War Criminals',
by Sir Hartley Shawcross

Justice Richard Goldstone: Address

The judgement of the International Military Tribunal at Nuremberg was delivered on Monday, 30th September 1946. That Tribunal was given the power by the victorious nations after the Second World War to try and punish persons who had committed Crimes against Peace, War Crimes and Crimes against Humanity as defined in its Charter.

Virtually the whole of humankind was of the view that crimes of the magnitude and bestiality of those committed by the Nazi regime would never be repeated. It was the view of most observers that the crimes were unique and a horrible deviation on the road of civilisation. That view proved not to be correct.

Crimes against peace, war crimes and crimes against humanity, including genocide, mass rape, torture, disappearances, forced removals and many other human rights violations have occurred repeatedly, on four continents, in the years since that judgement was delivered in this city. The hope of 'Never Again' has become the reality of 'Again and Again'. People in every country have to ask themselves and their leaders why this century has witnessed the death of 160 million people in wars – a ghastly statistic. What went wrong and is the 21st century to be a repeat?

One of the few beacons to shine out of the 20th Century is the Trial of the Major War Criminals at Nuremberg. The trials of Nuremberg – and at Tokyo – served a number of important ends. They ensured that guilt was personalised – when one looks at the emotive photographs of the accused in the dock at Nuremberg one sees a group of criminals. One does not see a group representative of the German people – the people who produced Goethe or Heine or Beethoven. The Nuremberg Trials were a meaningful instrument for avoiding the guilt of the Nazis being ascribed to the whole German people. They were important not only in the immediate context of the Nazi regime. They had a much broader significance for humanity. This was the first time that a multinational court was established in order to apply international law. The concept of crimes against humanity made it easier for the international community to become involved in serious human rights violations committed within the borders of sovereign states.

Why did the UN Security Council act with regard to the former Yugoslavia and thereafter Rwanda? After all, it had failed to take a similar step in other egregious cases such as Cambodia and Iraq, to mention only two obvious cases. In my view, the reasons are not hard to find. In the first place, the conduct which galvanised the Security Council in respect of the former Yugoslavia was reminiscent of the Holocaust – ethnic cleansing and photographs which could have been taken in Nazi concentration camps. It was happening in Europe and that had become inconceivable in the post-Nuremberg era. Then the international media was present and able to witness, report and film the events in question. They were seen by hundreds of millions of people all over the world.

The case of Rwanda was easier. In the first place the precedent had been created. Secondly, Rwanda was a member of the Security Council and the Government which had been instrumental in bringing the massacres to an end had itself requested the establishment of the Tribunal.

To date, the Tribunal for the former Yugoslavia has issued indictments in which over 50 alleged war criminals have been named. They include Radovan Karadzic, the President of the Bosnian Serb administration in Pale, Ratko Mladic, the commander of the army of the Bosnian Serb administration, and Milan Martic, the president of the former Croatian Serb administration in Knin.

There are 16 counts against Karadzic and Mladic. They include Genocide and Crimes against Humanity, and other war crimes. The counts relate to events which occurred between April 1992 and May 1995. They include the persecution of many hundreds of thousands of Bosnian Croat civilians. This includes unlawful confinement, murder, rape, sexual assault, torture, beating and robbery. They include the unlawful deportation and transfer of civilians, the unlawful shelling of civilians and, especially over a period of years in the city of Sarajevo, the destruction of homes and businesses and the destruction of places of worship.

On television and radio stations, in universities and schools in tens of countries, because of the tribunals, people are talking about war crimes.

The prosecution of war crimes in the former Yugoslavia and Rwanda, I hope, will be seen with hindsight to have been the beginning of a new era of enforcement of international humanitarian law.

The success of these tribunals will, to a large extent, determine if and when a permanent international criminal court will be established by the international community.

From the address by Judge R.J. Goldstone,
Prosecutor at the UN War Crimes Tribunals
for the former Yugoslavia and Rwanda,
at the conference on
'Human Rights Crimes Before the Law',
Nuremberg, September, 1995.

APPENDIX

NOTES ON THE DEFENDANTS

Hermann Goering

Goering's surrender was typical. He arrived laden with jewellery, joy and a trunkful of paracodeine pills – the entire German stock of the drug; and since the drug was unknown outside Germany, that means the entire world supply of paracodeine. He greeted his captors jovially, accepted the Army's contention that he was a prisoner of war, and gladly surrendered his valuable baton, the symbol of his marshalship . . .

. . . He carried gold cigar and cigarette cases, gold pens and pencils, and four jewelled watches and travelling clocks in his baggage. Everything he had was of the finest quality – and most of it had come from the occupied countries . . .

. . . In his final suicide, Goering carried out his ideals to the very end. He had faced the International Tribunal with courage but denied its right to judge or sentence him. In his last moments of life, he took matters into his own hands and, once again the dominant figure, cheated the hangman of the Allied Nations.

from 'Twenty-Two Cells in Nuremberg', by Douglas M. Kelly
(American psychologist at Nuremberg)
published by W.H. Allen, 1947

On 20 May 1945, in the sky-blue uniform of the Luftwaffe, Hermann Goering, the Number Two in the German hierarchy, swaggered in. He was brought to my office perspiring profusely. With the blubber of high living wobbling under his jacket, he presented a massive figure. He was weighed and the scales registered 264 lb.

The accused were seated meticulously in the order in which they appeared in the indictment. In the first few minutes

Goering began the extroverted, flamboyant play-acting that was to go on throughout the trial. He lounged with one fat arm spread out behind his thin neighbour, Hess, the other elbow hanging over the edge of the dock. Then he would loll forward, elbows on the barrier of the wooden dock in front . . .

from 'The Infamous of Nuremberg', by Colonel Burton Andrus, Commandant of Nuremberg Prison during the trial

Goering looks like the Queen in *Alice*.

Francis Biddle, US Judge on the Tribunal

Goering I remember even more vividly. He never lost his arrogance and his willingness to defend the Nazi régime. He was very skilful with words; he was a natural born lawyer. He understood English, I think, although he worked through interpreters.

Bernard Meltzer, lawyer, from 'Eyewitness at Nuremberg', by Hilary Gaskin, Arms and Armour Press, 1990

Wilhelm Keitel

Keitel was undoubtedly an ideal assistant to Hitler; his conditioning to unquestioned obedience was absolute. For him there was no such thing as objecting to an order of the Commander-in-Chief. When I asked him how officers and gentlemen could have carried out the outrageous orders of Hitler, he said again and again, 'We can only receive orders and obey. It is hard for Americans to understand the Prussian code of discipline.'

In jail he worked hard at trying to understand the non-Prussian code; and by the time the trial ended, he said in open court: 'I did not see the limit which is set even for a soldier's performance of his duty.'

Keitel attributed the atrocities to the SS, and the disgrace of the Army to its connection with the fanatical elite corps which

Hitler set up outside the regular army organisation. He maintained that he, personally, knew nothing of any atrocities and that, if he had learned of them, he would have left the Party. Hitler, he said, had limited his knowledge to what needed to be known for the planning of military action.

from 'Twenty-two Cells in Nuremberg' by Douglas M. Kelly

Keitel gave the impression to all of us that he would make a fine First Sergeant. He would obey anything his commander said . . . He sees the honour of the German military profession disgraced by the trial, feels let down by the Führer to whom he gave unquestioning obedience. His ramrod appearance conceals a weak, dependent character.

Leslie Frewin, 1969

Keitel told the psychologist Colonel Dunn about the responsibilities of a soldier – to accept orders and obey, as well as to accept the fate of his men.

'The Infamous of Nuremberg', by Colonel Burton Andrus

Alfred Rosenberg

Alfred Rosenberg, the Nazi Party philosopher, was a tall, slender, flaccid, womanish creature whose appearance belied his fanaticism and cruelty.

. . . Ordinarily Rosenberg's face wore a somewhat mild and somnolent expression; but it came awake, alive, and flushed with excitement, when he discussed his theories or his major work, *Myth of the Twentieth Century*. This opus was the foundation of his prestige, a basic book of the Nazi Party, and the authority on all racial problems. In it he had delineated his theories, but in unbelievably obscure and hazy fashion . . .

. . . Rosenberg explained that he had always held the idea that the Jews should be transported, and he suggested Madagascar – a French possession, incidentally – as a likely resettlement area for American Jews. He excused the Germans for not transporting their Jews by saying this was made impossible by outside pressure, so they simply had to exterminate them.

from 'Twenty-two Cells in Nuremberg', by Douglas M. Kelly

Albert Speer

Speer certainly seemed a man of courage, of moral discrimination, when contrasted with most of his fellow defendants. This image was not tarnished for some people even by the evidence against him. Lady Maxwell-Fyfe, for instance, responded with admiration to his character and intelligence. She commented to Mervyn Griffith-Jones that Speer was surely the sort of man Germany would need in the future. Griffith-Jones replied by producing a length of bloodstained telephone wire, about ten feet long, which had been picked up at Krupp's and had been used to flog workers. The admirers of Speer, then and now, must always ask by what means Speer had accomplished an industrial miracle between 1942 and the end of the War.

from 'The Nuremberg Trial' by Ann and John Tusa,
BBC Books, 1983

The Lawyers

All the defendants were represented by German lawyers, many of whom were distinguished, and they all put up an adequate defence. That is not to say that the German team was as good as those for the prosecution. The most eminent Nazi lawyers were conspicuous by their absence. Some of the German lawyers were ex-Nazis, some were not. They were severely handicapped by the lack of professional staff and assistants to help them in research and other work preparatory to the trial. And, I am afraid, the prosecuting team hardly treated them as professional equals: the no-fraternisation policy was strictly adhered to. They tended to become rather second-class citizens and their position was not enviable.

Some were genuinely shocked by the terrible things brought out in evidence. Yet although some of the German advocates were better than others, I do not think any prisoner suffered through inadequacy of defence. I have met some of those advocates in happier circumstances since; one of them, Naval Judge Kranzbuehler, a most able man who would have reached distinction in any society, took part in a programme on German television with me in the 1980s: we met as equals with courtesy.

from 'Life Sentence: the Memoirs of Lord Shawcross',
published by Constable, 1996

NOTES ON THE EVIDENCE

Rudolf Hoess
Commandant of Auschwitz, defence witness

One of the ill-considered moves by the defence was the calling as a witness of Rudolf Hoess, who had been Commandant of the notorious Auschwitz concentration camp. Hoess was called in a half-hearted attempt to counter the charge of conspiracy by showing that the defendants did not know what happened in the concentration camps. Hoess did testify that the killings had been carried out in secret and that they were not part of a general conspiracy. His evidence was given to a court that became hushed with horror, for he described coldly and unemotionally the mass suffering and deaths, but at the same time the efficiency with which he personally had supervised the deaths of a million and a half innocent human beings.

from 'Life Sentence: the Memoirs of Lord Shawcross',
published by Constable, 1996

Hoess made his confession, not in philosophical justification of what he had done, but simply as the explanation of a loyal member of the Party – a follower of Hitler and of Himmler. In 1941 he was called to Berlin to confer with Himmler. Himmler told him that a decision of the greatest importance had been reached at the highest level. That decision was to exterminate European Jewry . . .

. . . Devoid of moral principle, he reacted to the order to slaughter human beings as he would have to an order to fell trees. It was his 'war task'. And it was sufficient to him that someone higher in authority in the Party had given him 'the order'. As Hoess testified: 'In view of all these doubts which I had, the only one and decisive argument was the strict order and the reason given for it by the Reichsführer Himmler.'

from 'Crimes Against Humanity'

Rudolf Hoess was hanged on April 16, 1947 in the grounds of Auschwitz, sentenced for the 'mass murder of 4 million prisoners in the camp'.

The Hossbach Memorandum

One document, vital to the prosecution case . . . was known as the Hossbach Memorandum, the notes made by Hitler's adjutant Colonel Hossbach, of a conference held in the Reich Chancellery in Berlin on 5 November 1937. This conference was a crucial element in the prosecution argument that Nazi leaders had conspired to wage aggressive war. Present at the meeting were the Minister for War (Blomberg), the commanders of the Army, Navy and Air Force (Fritsch, Raeder and Goering), and the Minister for Foreign Affairs (Neurath). From 4.15 pm to 8.30 pm they were harangued by Hitler with his views on foreign policy – a statement which he said should be viewed as his last will and testament. According to Colonel Hossbach's notes Hitler defined the main problem of Germany, a nation of 85 million people, as one of' 'living space' or '*lebensraum*'. To prevent 'sterility', 'tension' and above all to gain enough food, Germany must secure a 'greater living space'. 'It is not a case of conquering people, but of conquering agriculturally useful space' – and in Europe.

from 'The Nuremberg Trial' by John and Ann Tusa

As early as November 5 1937, the Führer addressed his commanders-in-chief and Foreign Minister at the Reich Chancery in Berlin. This, according to one of his military adjutants named Hossbach is what he said:

'The Führer stated initially that the subject-matter of today's conference was of such high importance that its detailed discussion *in other states* would certainly take place before the Cabinet, in full session. However, he, the Führer, had decided *not* to discuss this matter in the larger circle of the Reich Cabinet, because of its importance. His subsequent statements were the result of detailed deliberations and of the experience of his four and half years in Government; he desired to explain to those present his fundamental ideas on the possibilities and necessities of expanding our foreign policy and in the interests of a far-sighted policy he requested that his statements be looked upon in the case of his death as his last will and testament.'

He went on: 'The aim of the German policy is the security and the preservation of the nation and its propagation. This is consequently a problem of space.

'The German nation comprises 85 million people, who, because of the number of individuals and the compactness of habitation, form a homogeneous European racial body the like of which cannot be found in any other country. On the other hand it justifies the demand for larger living space more than for any other nation.'

from 'The Nuremberg Trial', by R.W. Cooper,
Penguin Books, 1947

Mme Vaillant Couturier,
a prisoner in Auschwitz, prosecution witness

This Block 25, which was the anteroom of the gas chamber, if one may so call it, is well known to me because at that time we had been transferred to Block 26 and our windows opened on the yard of Block 25. One saw stacks of corpses piled up in the courtyard, and from time to time a hand or a head would stir amongst the bodies trying to free itself; it was a dying woman attempting to get free and live . . .

. . . The Jewish women, when they arrived in the first months of pregnancy, were subjected to abortion. When their pregnancy was near the end, after confinement, the babies were drowned in a bucket of water . . .

. . . We saw the unsealing of the coaches and the soldiers letting men, women and children out of them. We then witnessed heart-rending scenes, old couples forced to part from each other, mothers made to abandon their young daughters, since the latter were sent to the camp whereas mothers and children were sent to the gas chambers. All these people were unaware of the fate awaiting them. They were merely upset at being separated but they did not know that they were going to their death. To render their welcome more pleasant at this time – June, July 1944 – an orchestra composed of internees – all young and pretty girls, dressed in little white blouses and navy blue skirts – played, during the selection on the arrival of the trains, gay tunes such as *The Merry Widow*, the *Bacarolle* from *The Tales of Hoffman*, etc.

They were then informed that this was a labour camp, and since they were not brought into the camp they only saw the small platform surrounded by flowering plants. Naturally, they could not realise what was in store for them.

from the transcripts of the Nuremberg Trials